LEARNING ALLIANCES

Tapping into talent

David Clutterbuck

INSTITUTE OF PERSONNEL AND DEVELOPMENT

First published in 1998

Design by Paperweight
Typeset by
Fakenham Photosetting Ltd, Fakenham, Norfolk NR21 8NL
Printed in Great Britain by
The Cromwell Press, Wiltshire

British Library Cataloguing in Publication Data
A catalogue record for this book is available from the
British Library

ISBN 0-85292-749-5

INSTITUTE OF PERSONNEL
AND DEVELOPMENT

IPD House, Camp Road, London SW19 4UX
Tel: 0181 971 9000   Fax: 0181 263 3333
Registered office as above. Registered Charity No. 1038333
A company limited by guarantee. Registered in England No. 2931892

CONTENTS

Foreword   vii

1   THE ROLES PEOPLE PLAY   1

Helping others to learn – A role-map of helping to learn –
What about the learner? – Conclusion

2   THE COACH   18

Defining and describing a coach – The skills of an
effective coach – *Ten tips for giving feedback* – Four
coaching styles – Stepping in and stepping out –
Conclusion

3   THE GUARDIAN   36

The role of the guardian – The empowering guardian –
How the guardian seeks reward for his or her efforts –
Four styles of guardian – Managing guardian styles –
Conclusion

4   THE WORKPLACE COUNSELLOR   53

Defining and describing a counsellor – What is workplace
counselling? – Dimensions of counselling – The skills of
an effective counsellor at work – Psychometrics and
counselling – Conclusion

5   THE NETWORKER/FACILITATOR   70

Defining and describing a networker/facilitator – The
nature of networks – Learning networks – Four styles of

networker/facilitator – The skills of an effective
networker/facilitator – Conclusion

6   MENTORING: THE INTEGRATING ROLE   87

Definitions and models of mentoring – What do mentors
do? – Mentoring and learning styles – Who makes an
effective mentor? – Who makes an effective mentee? –
Managing the mentoring programme – Managing the
mentoring relationship – *Case-study: The reluctant
mentee* – What goes wrong with mentoring programmes?
– What goes wrong with mentoring relationships? –
Power in the mentoring relationship – The special case
of mentoring at the top – *Check-list for HR directors:
using professional mentors* – The integrative role of
mentoring – Conclusion

7   LEARNING ALLIANCES WITHIN THE
DEVELOPMENT FRAMEWORK   119

The styles and goals of mentoring – Managing the
development framework – The impact on human
resources – Conclusion

Appendix 1: Power in the mentoring relationship   135

Appendix 2: Sources of further information   140

FOREWORD

Coaching, mentoring, career counselling, tutoring, teaching, buddying, facilitating – the language of helping others to learn is replete with words and phrases that seem to overlap and that have widely different meanings to different people. The rapid evolution and increasing variety of styles of development alliance is a natural consequence of the widespread recognition that organisations and people survive in the modern world by continuously learning and by applying what they have learned.

Yet the confusing array of helping methods often leaves organisations and individuals bewildered. How much responsibility should I take for my own career and learning, and how much should I look to my employer for? Do I need a coach or a mentor? Or both? How would I recognise the difference anyway? How do I know if they are any good at helping me? And what do I as the learner have to do to get the most out of any developmental relationship?

The aim of this book is to answer these and many similar questions. Over more than 20 years of study and practical experience, it has increasingly become clear to me that employers and individuals – both learners and those who help them – require an integrating framework to make sense of the diversity of helping relationships and situations. The models presented in this book have evolved over a number of years, in discussion with literally thousands of managers around the world. With each evolution they increase in robustness and clarity.

If you are a manager who wants to contribute more to your organisation by helping develop the talent of other people, you should at a minimum acquire from your reading here some insights into how to adapt your style and behaviour more appropriately to the changing needs of learners. If you are a human resource professional, you should find at least some of the concepts and models presented of value in structuring more comprehensive, more effective support systems for organisational and individual learning.

In the end, however, learning by reading is not enough to make change happen. If you want to get real value from this book, go and experiment with the ideas, to see how they work for you and your organisation. Take some risks – step into the unknown, and compare what happens with the frameworks for learning that you will find in the following pages. Be bold, be open and sensitive, be honest with yourself and others. Who knows where it will take you and them?

David Clutterbuck

1   THE ROLES PEOPLE PLAY

Helping others to learn

The gap between what managers think and say they ought to do and what they *really* do has been expanding dramatically in recent years. More complex operating environments and broader responsibilities, and changing expectations from the organisation, the marketplace, direct reports and the managers themselves have made it easier – and sometimes essential – to fudge how they spend their time. What is clear is that most managers will more or less cheerfully admit that they spend too much time in meetings, that they are always under time pressures and that they don't spend enough time developing other people. What they are often more reluctant to admit is that they do very little strategic thinking, as opposed to tactical responding, and that they are not very good at developing themselves.

A panoply of appraisal systems, 360-degree feedback, personal development planning and other tools has had remarkably little effect – other, perhaps, than to make managers feel guiltier, in the knowledge of their shortcomings in developing themselves and others. While most accept intellectually the need to balance task, team and individual, it is hard to resist the undercurrent that sweeps the manager day by day out towards the task issues. After all, these are typically the most immediate, the easiest to resolve rationally, the most comfortable to deal with, and the most visible to the manager's own bosses. They are also, often, the issues that are most readily measured and measurable.

Combined with the gradual movement towards larger spans of control, and towards short-term project groups where the manager has little opportunity to get to know the team intimately, it is not surprising that many managers are becoming increasingly remote from their direct reports. At an IPD conference in 1995, some 250 human resource professionals were asked who they learned from at work most frequently and most intensively. On neither score did managers come out well. Some people scarcely saw their managers from one week to the next. The most frequent source of learning, overwhelmingly, was the person's peers; and the most intensive, a mentoring relationship, outside the line. Dozens of workshops with managers at all levels and in all disciplines have since confirmed the general pattern as regards the line manager's role.

This book begins, therefore, with a number of assumptions about learning at work:

□ The manager who is in control of his or her own learning is more likely to be an effective and frequent developer of others.

□ The notion that all managers should be coaches, while laudable, is far too limiting; sheer practicality demands that they become *facilitators* of learning – creating an environment where 'helping to learn' is a task shared among many heads, both within and outside the team, rather than assuming the whole role themselves. (This includes the potential for the team to have an active role in helping the manager to learn.)

□ Just as many people can play a part in developing others, so there are many roles they can play. These roles come by many names, often confusingly ('mentor', 'coach' and 'counsellor' often carry widely differing meanings, depending on where and how they are applied).

The aim of this chapter is to provide an overarching dynamic to understand how these many roles fit, both with each other and within the broad framework of development in a learning organisation.

Helping others to learn is an integral part of every manager's job. But what does that actually mean? Until recent years, a typical answer would have been that it was the manager or supervisor's job to show direct reports how to do things, and to appraise them periodically to direct their attention to areas of competence where learning was needed, for them to achieve their task objectives. This was never really adequate, even then, for busy managers have for centuries made use of 'sitting by Nellie' – assigning competent workers the additional task of helping newcomers to learn. It is even less so in the empowering flatter structures that most companies aspire to (or at least pay lip-service to).

The reality today is that the line manager increasingly needs to be a *facilitator* of learning. This is a very different role from team coach, although team coach may be part of it. The facilitator of learning creates *the climate, in which the maximum relevant learning can take place*. Part of this is about the manager's behaviour, encouraging people to ask questions and take responsibility for their own learning; part about the kind of structures the team was to promote, capture, share and apply learning. In a recent 11-company study I conducted with Hertfordshire TEC into the nature of The Learning Team,[1] the conclusions included:

- Learning goals usually lose out to task goals – unless the team has very effective systems to redress the balance.
- Different types of team (the study identifies five) have different learning dynamics – each requiring a different approach to managing learning.
- The more types of team people are exposed to, the greater the transfer of learning between and within teams.
- Effective learning teams encourage their members to adopt specific learning roles on behalf of the team.

The facilitator of learning recognises that the team members are often as knowledgeable about the performance of team tasks as he or she is. He or she allows the team to have reflective space, in which learning can be reviewed, and provides a counterbalance to the instinct to focus entirely on getting things done, rather than thinking about what needs to be done and how. He or she encourages constructive dissent – perhaps casting individuals temporarily into the 'stranger' role in order to help the group recognise issues they are avoiding, consciously or unconsciously – and opens up discussion with people outside the team to ensure that the team maintains a window on the world. He or she encourages individuals to set and achieve learning goals and to link those with the learning goals of the team itself.

By making the learning process largely self-sustained and managed within the team, facilitators of learning create the mental space to think critically about their wider helping role. Formally or informally they become off-line mentors to people outside their team. They become increasingly adept at educating their own line bosses. They become important gateways in networks of influence and information, sharing knowledge by linking people to each other. And they also develop a healthy attitude towards their own learning, providing a role model of how to set and work towards personal learning goals.

An important part of this is recognising the potential to learn from all those around them. One of the most useful exercises I undertake with managers is to persuade them to describe their own *learning net* – the people around them from whom they can usefully learn. Invariably, the learning net is much wider than they think, and the efficiency with which they extract learning from others is fairly low. One of the most common insights for many of these managers is that they need to spend less time coaching their direct reports and more time asking 'What can you teach me?' Team meetings take on a whole new dimension when participants expect to share personal learning and help educate their manager.

Equally important – and the core of this book – is the notion of the *learning alliance*. In essence, the learning alliance is just one strand in the learning net. But this particular strand is greatly reinforced by a stronger sense of learning purpose: an understanding between the two people that this is a proactive relationship, valued by both of them. The very word 'alliance' implies some form of benefit to both parties. Most frequently and powerfully seen in mentoring, mutuality of benefit occurs in all development alliances and is, to a greater or lesser extent, the glue that holds them together. The benefit to the helper may be as simple as feeling gratified that someone else is interested in tapping into their experience, so reinforcing their sense of self-worth. Or it may be much more down to earth – for example, being able to delegate tasks so you can get on with more important or challenging tasks instead.

The learning alliance brings a host of benefits to the people within it and to the organisation itself.

Among them:

☐ Learning alliances reinforce attempts to push the primary responsibility for developing others back to the manager, where it belongs, and through the manager, to the team as a whole.

☐ HR is able to concentrate far more on supporting learning, rather than providing it.

☐ HR is able to take a more objective perspective on training and development in general.

☐ Line managers are better able to define the development needs of their teams, because they experience people's views and concerns first-hand.

☐ Employees are more realistic about their expectations of help in development (they learn to think beyond courses to a much wider range of options).

☐ Learning alliances are cost-effective: they typically develop both partners.

☐ Learning solutions can be personalised to a far greater extent than is ever possible through training. Development alliances combine the immediacy and timeliness with personal relevance and emotional support – something no other development solution can achieve.

☐ Development alliances provide the thin end of the wedge to switch top management on to self-development. By learning to help others, they often rediscover how to learn, themselves.

A role-map of helping to learn

In a recent international study of long-term high-performing companies[2] it emerged that companies sustain high levels of competitive advantage in large part through the sensitivity with which they handle critical balances between apparent opposites. These balances range from the immediately obvious, such as between control and autonomy, and the less obvious, such as the need to generate pride in the company and its products yet to be sufficiently humble to listen and empathise with a wide range of stakeholders.

Among the key generic balances was between the 'soft' and 'hard' sides of people management. High-performing companies are 'tough but fun'; they combine very demanding targets and an intolerance of repeated failure with a remarkable degree of personal support. We called this apparent conflict 'challenge versus nurturing'. Challenge is closely related to the intellectual/rational values of the organisation; nurturing to the emotional values. An effective human is a combination of intellectual and emotional processes, with the brain acting as a continuous arbiter between the two, both consciously and unconsciously. Precisely the same is true of the organisation: the ability to manage both the intellectual and the emotional interpretation and reaction to external stimuli is a defining characteristic of functional excellence.

Figure 1
TWO DIMENSIONS OF DEVELOPMENT

The emphasis the company places on these alternatives will tend to determine the kind of help it offers people. A highly rational organisation-centred approach will tend not to place a great deal of emphasis on stress management, for example. But it might pay a lot of attention to succession-planning. A company with a leaning towards the rational and towards individual development might emphasise the setting of stretching goals for its people. One with more of an interest in individual development and emotional support might provide career counselling. And one that leans more towards organisation development and emotional support might spend a lot of effort managing employee communication in order to reinforce people's understanding of and commitment to the business vision.

In practice, all these areas are important in managing both individual and organisational development and learning. However, most companies have a tendency to emphasise some areas of the diagram more than others, often by default rather than by design. Assessing the desired emphasis against the actual can be a useful step in aligning developmental provision with business and individual needs.

When we come to individual relationships within the learning process, a modified version of the same basic model helps explain the key behavioural options. The challenging–nurturing/rational–emotional dimension remains. In place of an organisation v individual focus, however, we can consider the spectrum from directive to non-directive. Directive behaviours, at their extreme, would involve a more senior/experienced person in:

☐ deciding what learning should take place, when and how – setting the learning goals and the path towards achieving them

☐ taking the lead in discussions

☐ giving feedback from his or her own observations.

Non-directive behaviours, on the other hand, put the learner in the driving seat. The learner sets the agenda, initiates and steers discussions, and gains his or her own insights, with the help of the more experienced person. A learner who is sufficiently mature to operate in this way is afforded much greater potential to carry out personal transformation. One recent study of mentoring relationships in Norway[3] found that the most successful relationships were those in which the mentee was most active and the mentor least active.

In practice, effective development alliances function between the extremes of these dimensions. Each quadrant of the model defines a 'helping to learn' role or a different form of learning alliance:

☐ The directive/challenging quadrant (A) involves a number

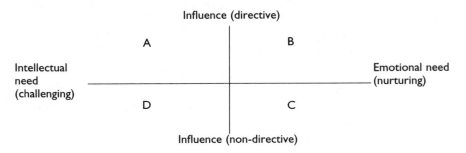

Figure 2
DIMENSIONS OF MENTORING

of behaviours that can best be clustered together under the heading COACH. At one extreme, the traditional style of coaching involved giving people a task, watching them perform it, giving them feedback on how they performed, and reviewing with them how to do better next time. This was (and still is in many organisations) a relatively directive activity. It was more or less challenging according to how big a step the task represented. More modern concepts of coaching emphasise dialogue, ownership of the issue by the learner, and allowing the learner to provide much of his or her own feedback. However, the learner still does not own or manage the *process*, which depends on the observational and questioning skills of the coach.

☐ The directive/nurturing quadrant (B) holds a set of behaviours that can be described as GUARDIAN. At one extreme lies the corporate sponsor or godfather figure who may help people learn by ensuring they are included on high-profile, high-learning-exposure projects or teams. This individual may also *hinder* the learners' development by becoming a guru, or by protecting them from the consequence of mistakes, and so on. More typically, he or she will be a source of advice, a role model and a general guide through political and practical aspects of learning to function effectively within an organisation.

☐ The nurturing/non-directive quadrant (C) is conveniently labelled COUNSELLOR. Counselling is a learner-centred method of giving someone support. We know from many studies that people learn best when they have the right environment and the right frame of mind – counselling supports the learning process by helping people examine and come to terms with their own fears, motivations and blocks to progress.

☐ The challenging/non-directive quadrant (D) defines the NETWORKER/FACILITATOR role. Here the goal is to make learners as self-reliant as possible, as quickly as possible. The networker side of the role helps the learners expand their circle of information and influence resources, both within and outside the organisation. The facilitator side of the role helps them think through how to take increasing charge of their own learning and development, continuously expanding the range of learning resources on which they can draw.

Within each of these four broad roles, the more experienced partner has considerable freedom to operate in a more or less directive, more or less challenging/nurturing style, according to the need of the learner. Indeed, the capability of the coach, counsellor, facilitator or networker will depend to a large extent on his or her ability to make these adjustments in a continuous and timely manner.

One critical role has been left out, however: that of mentor. A mentor is not a coach *per se* (of which more later), nor is the role synonymous with any of the other 'helping to learn' roles. The answer, quite simply, is that the mentor's role draws on all of these. The behavioural map of helping to learn can be expanded to include a wide variety of specific behaviours, as shown in Figure 3.

Where you draw the line around mentoring depends on whether you adopt a traditional US definition of *career-oriented* mentoring (having a powerful sponsor) or the European definition of *developmental* mentoring (where the prime focus is personal growth and learning). However, most organisations I have worked with in Europe draw the line as shown in Figure 3. The diamond represents the boundaries of the mentor's behaviours and hence of the role itself. So what distinguishes mentoring from other 'helping to learn' roles is

Figure 3
THE BEHAVIOURAL MATRIX

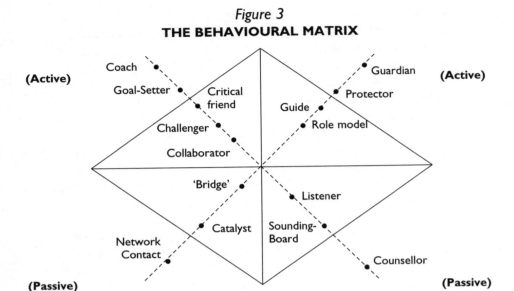

the requirement to be able to operate in all of the others, moving from one to the other at need. The effective mentor therefore needs to have skills as both coach *and* counsellor, facilitator *and* networker. Whether that makes mentoring a higher level of skill, or simply a different combination of skills is debatable. What is clear, however, is that the more roles a manager is able to operate in, and the more readily he or she is able to switch between them, the more effective the manager is likely to be in those roles.

Another useful way of looking at the difference between roles in helping others to learn is by comparing learning situations, as in Table 1. At school or university, the primary learning situation is the lecture. The role of the teacher, in stereotype, is to provide facts and test the learner's retention and understanding of them. With the exception of school-girl/boy crushes, this is rarely a close relationship and its objective is less the applicability of the learning itself than the passing of an examination. The nature of the learning, then, is narrow rather than holistic, explicit rather than tacit, reported rather than experienced. (In practice, good teachers do much more than that, but they do so because they are able to step outside the strict teaching role into some or all of the roles we look at next.) The relationship is always one of superior to inferior because the teacher has rank in age, status and subject knowledge.

The tutor–student relationship marks a shift away from being told to being asked to work it out for oneself. Dissenting opinion is encouraged (within limits – it is not often productive to rubbish your professor's lifetime work!) and at post-graduate level, at least, the learner often becomes more knowledgeable than the tutor in the narrow subject of study, especially at advanced degree level. The content of learning in a tutorial relationship is heavily biased towards knowledge rather than skill: the ability to apply knowledge in the real world (for example, for business school lecturers to be able to run a company) is not essential. Indeed, business schools have over the years shown themselves in a number of cases to be remarkably inept at running commercial ventures.

Coaching, on the other hand, does demand some practical experience – been there, seen it, done it – if not of the actual task, of tasks sufficiently similar to transfer understanding. The coach need not be more expert than the learner – witness the top sports coaches and their charges. Coaching is less about acquiring knowledge than about acquiring the skills to apply knowledge. It makes performance explicit, in order for the learner to manage improvement. Done well, it combines extrinsic and intrinsic feedback to motivate and inform the learner's practice towards a clear performance goal. Coaching often slides into mentoring when discussion and dialogue move onto wider, more personal issues.

Mentoring is different again. It focuses not on tasks or skills but on the transfer of intuitive and tacit knowledge. It often results in very close personal friendships, although that is not always the case. In developmental mentoring, there is minimal expression of or influence from the more senior partner's status – it is a relationship of equals. (In career mentoring – where to be fair the primary objective is not learning – the opposite is true; the senior partner's power and influence are a major part of the attraction for the more junior partner.) Most important of all, effective mentoring is a two-way learning experience: the mentors frequently learn as much or more than the mentees.

Table 1
COMMON LEARNING METHODS: THE ROLE DIFFERENCES

	Teacher	Tutor	Coach	Mentor	Counsellor
Nature of transfer	Information with some knowledge Explicit	Knowledge Mainly explicit	Skill, some knowledge Mainly explicit	Wisdom Mainly implicit	Self-awareness, insight Making the implicit explicit
Direction of learning	Teacher to pupil	Mainly tutor to student, but sometimes moderately two-way	Coach to learner	Two-way	Mostly one-way
Power distance	High	Moderately high	Moderately low, depending on work relationship	Low	Low (but potential for abuse is high)
Nature of feedback	Impersonal – marks and scores Provided entirely by teacher	Personal, questioning processes Provided mainly by tutor	Personal, questioning performance Provided mainly by the coach	Personal, provided by the learner	Avoids direct feedback, but encourages learner to review own issues
Intensity of the personal relation ship	Usually low	Low to moderate	Moderate but can develop into high friendship	Moderate to high	Minimal personal involvement

Counselling does not fit easily into this list because no formal transfer of learning takes place. That is not to say that counselling is unimportant as a learning role – far from it. But counselling works by fostering learning about oneself. It is therefore an essential stepping-stone to acquiring task knowledge (tutoring), skills (coaching) and intuitive understanding of organisations and systems (mentoring) – but not part of the same hierarchy of methods.

What about the learner?

So much for the roles and behaviours of the person helping others to learn. But a learning partnership involves at least two people. What about the roles and behaviours of the learner? Clearly, there is a significant degree of cause and effect between the behaviour of the two parties. The learner who is consciously or unconsciously seeking a guru who will provide all the answers to his or her problems will probably find one (or the illusion of one). It can be very seductive to a manager to receive this kind of admiration and regard, and oh so easy to slip into playing the guru role.[4]

Understanding the learner's behaviours – and helping the learner to behave appropriately – is an essential part of this increasingly complex dynamic. Double-loop learning[5] will always be more effective than single-loop.

The chapters that follow will attempt to pull out the threads of the core model of development alliances, exploring how each role can be applied to the benefit of the individuals, the team and the organisation. Before they do so, however, it is worth taking a moment to consider why managers and others should *want* to help others learn. After all, although we often take it for granted that managers are pleased, even eager, to accept that role, the evidence of behaviour does not necessarily support such a view. If they were truly enthusiastic, surely they would make the management of learning a priority and set a significant proportion of their time each week aside for that purpose?

The evidence from the learning teams project and elsewhere suggests that there are three sets of factors at work in preventing managers from acting as facilitators of learning:

- □ outright hostility to helping others to learn
- □ lack of personal commitment to learning goals
- □ environmental issues, such as work (task) pressures.

Outright hostility is, fortunately, relatively rare. The manager who deliberately withholds information and does not want to see his or her people grow in capability is an anachronism who appears less and less. Such managers' motivations are various, but most typically revolve around wanting to protect their job and status, an excessive need to control what is going on, or an extreme impatience that allows them to convince themselves that it is always quicker to do things themselves than to spend time helping someone else to gain the skills and experience.

Much more insidious – and more common – is the manager who has largely given up on his or her own continued learning and for whom helping others to learn is a chore. The opportunity to learn from direct reports, peers and other people has few attractions to such managers – they can't see the point.

Both of these types of manager are swift to seize upon work pressures to justify their lack of enthusiasm and interest in developing others. It is easy to do so because even in the best-managed teams there will always be a pressure for task objectives and activities to crowd out learning objectives and activities. The difference is that facilitators of learning *create* the time, both for themselves and for others in the team, to support each other in their learning. They often do so in spite of severe practical difficulties. For example, I have encountered a number of factories where lean production means that teams are so slim they cannot afford to release members for training. In those with managers who are not committed to facilitating learning, development virtually stops. In others, the manager and the team work together ingeniously to find all sorts of learning opportunities.

The result is that many people spend most of their working lives missing opportunities to learn. It is not just the workshop we could not attend, or the book we did not read, or the challenging project we did not put our name forward for. It is the continuous failure to tap into the views, perspective and knowledge of the people around us.

This failure to seek and maintain learning dialogue leads to all sorts of operational problems. The senior managers in a British factory in the food industry complained to me that they could not get the shop-floor employees to take the initiative or to take any responsibility for improving the production processes. When I spoke to the employees, they were unanimous in their enthusiasm for taking greater responsibility but were frustrated by the managers' apparent reluctance to let go.

What a remarkable opportunity for learning by both sides! Yet each side was reluctant to enter into dialogue with the other for fear of losing face or having to face up to disagreeable truths.

An important factor here is the creation of reflective space – time to focus on thinking, understanding and learning, instead of doing. Reflective space is important at three levels: personal (quiet thinking time on one's own); dyadic (one-to-one); and as a group or team. Observational and anecdotal evidence suggests that people need to take part at all three levels to take full advantage of the learning opportunities around them.

What happens in reflective space? It typically starts with the mind cluttered with all sorts of issues, concerns and thoughts. When the learner makes the transition into personal reflective space (PRS), he or she is usually responding to a learned trigger. For some (relatively few) people, this can simply be closing the office door and shutting the world out. For others, it can be a repetitious activity (for example, jogging, ironing, driving a familiar route home), a period of enforced inactivity (for example, on an aeroplane or train), or simply relaxing in the bath! However they achieve PRS, people find that the immediate first effect is to focus their thinking down on one issue for a period of quality time. Subconscious thinking they have already done now has an opportunity to surface: they are also able to 'step outside the box' and look at the issue more objectively than they have previously done. An 'inner dialogue' takes place, which people sometimes refer to as 'giving myself a good talking to'.

Rearranging the problem more clearly often leads to significant insight or understanding. This in turn allows the learner to reframe a problem in a way that makes it easier, or at least clearer, to deal with. Alternative solutions give way under examination to some specific actions that the learner can take.

One of the interesting aspects of PRS is the energy curve associated with it. Before going into PRS, people typically have a lot of externally expressed energy. The more reflective they become, the more that energy is focused internally. When they come out of PRS, they tend to have an explosion

Figure 4
PERSONAL REFLECTIVE SPACE

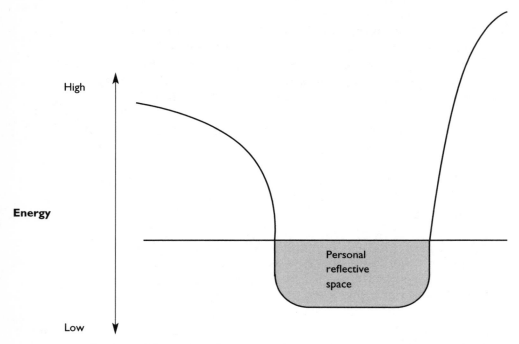

of external energy because they are eager to deal with the issue now that they understand it better.

Most of the development alliance takes place in dyadic reflective space (DRS) in which a learner and a helper work together to achieve developmental goals. DRS works in much the same way as PRS, but it adds external dialogue to the inner dialogue. The helper is able to provide another perspective, ask questions the learner had not considered, and draw on other experience. Done sensitively, this intrusion reinforces understanding and empowers the learner; done insensitively, it breaks the spell and may create dependence.

Conclusion

Learning alliances are complex, diverse and immensely powerful. However, they all make use of a range of behaviours that can be mapped according to the needs of the learner, the skills of the helper, and the context in which both operate.

The chapters that follow address in turn each of the five key roles of coach, guardian, counsellor, networker and mentor, explaining the differences between them and suggesting ways of increasing effectiveness in each role.

Together, these roles provide a mutually supportive cluster of one-to-one helping approaches which organisations can support and encourage.

End-notes

1 CLUTTERBUCK D. *The Learning Team Report*. St Albans, Hertfordshire TEC, 1998.

2 GOLDSMITH G. and CLUTTERBUCK D. *The Winning Streak Mark II*. London, Orion. 1997.

3 ENGSTROM T.E.J. and MYKLETUN R.J. 'Personality factors' impact on success in the mentor-protégé relationship'. Paper by Norwegian School of Hotel Management, 1997.

4 LEE, M. 'Playing the guru: inequality of personal power in relationships'. *Management Education and Development*, vol. 22 pt 4, pp302–309.

5 ARGYRIS C. and SCHON D. A. *Organisational Learning: A theory of action perspective*. Reading, Mass., Addison-Wesley, 1978.

2 THE COACH

Defining and describing a coach

As with all of the roles involved in helping others to learn, coaching can mean different things in different contexts. In particular, it is often confused with mentoring, so here may be a useful point at which to emphasise the essential differences between the two roles, as exemplified in Table 2:

Table 2
COACHING V MENTORING

Coaching	Mentoring
Concerned with task	Concerned with implications beyond the task
Focuses on skills and performance	Focuses on capability and potential
Primarily a line manager role	Works best off-line
Agenda set by or with the coach	Agenda set by the learner
Emphasises feedback *to* the learner	Emphasises feedback and reflection *by* the learner
Typically addresses a short-term need	Typically a longer-term relationship, often 'for life'
Feedback and discussion primarily explicit	Feedback and discussion primarily about implicit, intuitive issues and behaviours

Both coaching and mentoring are heavily dependent on providing sufficient personal reflective space for a learning dialogue to take place, and this is where the skills overlap between mentor and coach largely occurs. The difficulty in finding reflective space, and the basic lack of confidence many managers have in their ability to coach, probably account for the low standard of coaching reported in many companies. In particular, feedback, as an essential element of coaching, appears to be poorly done. A study by the US-based Conference Board identified inadequate personal feedback as

Figure 5
A LEARNER-CENTRED MODEL OF COACHING

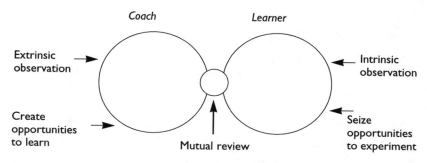

the top cause of employee performance problems in 60 per cent of European and North American companies studied. Another study, this time by the University of Missouri, found that salespeople rated their bosses lowest, out of a range of skills, on giving them useful feedback on performance.[1]

The movement in recent years to redefine coaching more as an activity based around the learner's agenda is a healthy step forward in sharing ownership of the learning process. However, it is as well to recognise that coaching is actually itself a spectrum of styles, and that effective coaches are able to move within that spectrum as circumstances (usually the learner's needs) demand.

Before we examine those styles, let's describe the coaching process overall. Coaching is a pragmatic approach to helping people manage their acquisition or improvement of skills. As Figure 6 indicates, there are five critical activities and these are shared between the coach and the learner.

1   *Identify learning opportunities* – Learning opportunities may be either serendipitous and experimental or planned and selective. Ideally, the regular developmental dialogue between line manager and team members identifies areas of development need, which may be formally recorded in personal development plans or simply retained in awareness. Both the coach/manager and the learner can seek opportunities for the learner to practise this skill, but the coach will tend to have greater influence and a wider perspective on where the opportunities might lie. Alternatively, both may be alert to

opportunities to experiment where the intended lesson is not clear but where the potential to stretch the learner is high. For example, inviting a learner to take the chair at a team briefing may both raise his or her confidence and reveal a whole new range of skills that can be worked on.

2   *Seize the learning opportunity* – The learner has to approach the task positively – albeit sometimes with trepidation – and an intention to learn. It may also be important for him or her to have at least some idea of what the expected lessons might be. The coach has a role here in motivating the learner to make the effort (sometimes to coax, although *coach* and *coax* surprisingly do not come from the same linguistic root) and to help him or her think through the learning objectives.

3   *Extrinsic feedback* – The coach observes how the learner tackles the task and compares against both previous attempts and an expected level of performance. He or she presents the feedback in a way that the learner will accept and that helps the learner focus on one or two key elements of the task at a time. The quality of the coach's observation is important here, but so is the ability to communicate what the coach has observed to the learner.

4   *Intrinsic feedback* – The learner observes what is happening as he or she carries out the task. This is often much harder than it sounds, and the coach can help a great deal by giving clues as to what to attend to. For example, an ice-skating or tennis coach will break down a jump or a swing into segments and help the learner 'listen' to what his or her muscles are doing at each point. The learner's level of competence grows as he or she develops greater and greater awareness of the details of posture, muscle tension and timing. After a while the learner can answer the question 'How do you think you did?' with his or her own, generally accurate, assessment of what felt right and wrong. The pace of learning typically increases rapidly at this point as conscious competence begins to kick in.

5   *Mutual review* – The core of the process is the creation of personal reflective space, in which the coach and the learner

can review what happened, draw appropriate lessons, and plan new learning opportunities. This is a demanding stage for both of them. It requires a high degree of openness, self-awareness, willingness to be self-critical, creativity and opportunistic planning.

The skills of an effective coach

Giving extrinsic feedback is a two-part skill. The first part demands a very high competence in observation. In reality, the term 'observation' is misleading because it implies only a visual monitoring, whereas good coaches also have to be effective listeners and empathisers. Recent studies of the mind and interpersonal behaviour[2] confirm that observation of others is an aspect of social competence ('emotional intelligence') that is more developed in some people than in others. The extent to which a manager is sensitive to the nuances of posture, expression, language and otherwise expressed feelings of others determines in large part how effective a coach he or she will be.

Equally, the emphasis upon which senses the coach uses will depend upon the nature of the learning to take place. When it comes to motor skills – for example, skiing or cricket, or learning to plaster walls – visual observation will be to the fore. But aural observation still plays an important role. Which is why, for example, coaches (called 'observers') for the Institute of Advanced Motorists ask learners to give a running commentary on the road conditions ahead. It allows the coach to assess what the learner does against what the learner thinks he or she is doing.

With behavioural issues it is more often what people say that has the greatest impact and will be easiest for the coach to observe. But body language and the physical reactions of others are also important clues to what is going on. It is also helpful wherever possible to place oneself in the learner's shoes: to develop genuine empathy. The effective coach senses feelings by seeing with the learner's eyes, hearing with the learner's ears, feeling with the learner's hands, and by sharing the learner's emotions – insofar as it is possible to do so as an observer. This talent is less a matter of innate or learned skill than of attitude, of interest in the learner's perspective.

Real time v remembered feedback

It is a truism that feedback is usually most useful and of greatest impact when it is delivered on the spot. This is not always practical in the work situation, but good coaches attempt to get as close to real time as possible. If the coaching dialogue has to take place after the event, it may help to encourage learners to acquire the habit of recording their intrinsic feedback as near to the event as possible. Video feedback can also be a useful method, particularly for improving motor skills.

So much has been written about giving feedback elsewhere that I hesitate to discuss the topic in detail. The *Ten Tips* below provide a succinct summary of some of the accumulated wisdom on feedback.

Ten tips for giving feedback

1 Make it timely. The closer to the observed behaviour, the easier for learners to put themselves 'back into the frame' and match your extrinsic feedback against their own intrinsic observations.

2 Check the learners' understanding of the purpose of the feedback. Are you trying to help them understand, to give them encouragement, or to tick them off? Clarity of purpose makes it much easier for a learner to put the feedback into context and respond appropriately. Many a well-meant intervention by a coach results in a retreat under fire as the learner misinterprets his or her intentions.

3 Let the learner speak first. Intrinsic feedback should always have pride of place because the learner has already accepted that data. The coach can then build on the learner's observations with additional feedback that leads to greater understanding.

4 Own the feedback. Offering second-hand feedback can be like selling second-hand underwear: most people would find it hard not to feel insulted. Wherever possible, the

coach should base comments on personal observation. If another person's view is pertinent, then ideally the coach should arrange for the observations to be given direct. (Some of the most valuable feedback I have had at sports has been when my coach asks a 12-year-old, more accomplished than I am, to observe and comment!)

5 Make it positive and private. Whether you are a beginner or a world champion, almost all performance feedback is 'negative' in the sense that it identifies areas for improvement. Equally, almost all performance feedback is 'positive' in that it presents an opportunity to progress and do things better. The more the coach can lean towards the optimistic, the more motivational the feedback will be and the more easily the learner will accept and internalise it. The psychological environment is also influenced by the physical environment: choosing the right place to give feedback is as important as choosing the right time.

6 Select priority areas. Effective coaches observe a great deal that could be improved. But they feed back to the learner only a fraction of what they observe. They recognise that too much feedback can paralyse the learner; too little leaves him or her unsure of what to do next. Judging the right quantity of feedback and concentrating on the most urgent areas for improvement is a critical skill.

7 Be specific. The vaguer the feedback, the less use the learner can make of it. 'You didn't carry that meeting with you, did you?' is of much less value than 'You lost the confidence of the team at three points during the meeting – when you let John hijack the discussion on relocation, when you let the debate run on too long, and when you didn't step in to force a decision.' (In practice, the effective coach would encourage the learner to draw out these observations themselves – see point 3.)

8 Offer alternatives. The learner can feel much more in control if he or she is able to make key decisions on how the dialogue should progress. For example, in seeking explanation for behaviour or for a task outcome, the

coach can suggest a variety of options, encourage the learner to add others, then encourage the learner to sift through those options to reach his or her own conclusions. The same applies to options for action – what to do next. If the coach feels that a selected option is 'wrong', he or she can either suggest the learner tries it, to see what happens, or pose more questions that oblige the learner to think about the issue from alternative perspectives.

9 Support action. If ownership of the process is to be shared, then the coach must accept some responsibility for the actions the learner takes as a result of the coaching dialogue. At the very least, he or she should provide encouragement. It may also be appropriate to provide some specific help – for example, offering to read a report before it goes to the learner's manager.

10 How do you sound? Effective feedback is two-way. It is important for the coach's development to be aware of how he or she comes across to the learner. In practice, this may mean reversing the roles: the coach devotes time and effort to intrinsic observation of his or her own coaching behaviour and style, and invites the learner to provide feedback on the coaching process as the learner has experienced it. Above all, when giving feedback, *think what it says about you.*

In giving critical or 'negative' feedback, it helps to have some down-to-earth principles to work to. Effective coaches typically challenge:

- the behaviour, not the person
- the learner's assumptions, not his or her intellect
- the learner's perceptions, not his or her judgement
- the learner's values, not his or her value (ie sense of personal worth or self-esteem).

The objective in each case is to enhance learners' understanding and to introduce realism without making them feel diminished or threatened. This does not mean, however, that the good coach never shouts at the learner: I often find a loud bellow of 'Shoulders!' or 'Knees!' by my sports coach a useful and forceful reminder. But he or she must be careful never to do so in a denigrating or embarrassing manner. (My coach knows I'm thick-skinned enough not to worry about startled looks from other people!)

Bite-sized learning

Effective coaches understand the task or issue sufficiently clearly from their own experience and observation to break it down into smaller chunks that are more easily addressed. Take two examples: a physical skill, such as a jump on ice, and a knowledge-work task, such as project management. With the physical skill, the coach might break it into the run-up in preparation, where the athlete gains the speed necessary to jump; the pre-jump position; the lift-off; the position in-air; the landing; and the position immediately post-landing. The coach may choose to concentrate on the first elements and work forward, or on the final elements and work backward, or on one or two elements that need particular attention. Working forward enables the learner to understand how the sequence of actions fits together, and tends to be most appropriate when the learner is a beginner at the task. Working backward from the outcome can be more motivating, because the learner can more clearly visualise success. This tends to be more effective when the learner has already grasped the basics. Recognising where to focus the learner's attention at the right time is a fundamental skill for a sports coach.

The same principles apply to knowledge, tasks or behaviours. All tasks at work can be broken down into algorithms – step-by-step processes to achieve a defined outcome. Unlike the sporting analogy, however, it is not always possible to repeat them over and over for improvement. The learning has to take place while the employee works through the task, perhaps over weeks or months. By understanding the steps within the task, exploring with the learner about how he or she will tackle each step, and reviewing the process and outcomes of each step, the coach helps to maximise the learning that takes place. Working backwards is not normally a practical option, but the coach can help the learner do so in his or her imagination, visualising the outcomes and how the learners' handling of each step along the way will contribute to them.

Questions *not* answers

Most training courses for coaches nowadays emphasise the importance of asking questions, to stimulate the learner's own thinking, rather than giving answers. In practice, as we shall explore shortly, this can be a rather narrow view which fails to recognise the variety of situations in which a coach may operate. Nonetheless, it is not possible to coach effectively without having very good questioning skills.

Using appropriate questions is critical for a variety of reasons:

☐ It includes the learner more firmly in the process.
☐ It gives an opportunity for the coach to observe and listen.
☐ It allows a gradual peeling off of layers of awareness and understanding by the learner.
☐ It helps to make implicit issues explicit, by obliging the learner to articulate what he or she thinks is happening or has happened.
☐ It enables the coach to check that the learner understands the task and the circumstances in which the task has to be done.

However, there is a negative side to questioning, too:

☐ Overused, it can distance the coach too far from the issue.
☐ It can uncover only what the learner is already either consciously aware of or has observed unconsciously – no input, no output.
☐ The pattern of questions often assumes a life and logic of its own; it is all too easy for the coach to impose his or her own agenda, leading the learner to a set of conclusions different from what might have been the case with a more open menu of questions.
☐ Excessive use of questions by the coach can discourage a learner from asking questions (especially if the coach responds with more questions and no answers).

Figure 6
THE QUESTIONING CYCLE FOR COACHING

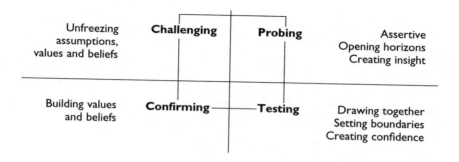

Unfreezing assumptions, values and beliefs	**Challenging**	**Probing**	Assertive Opening horizons Creating insight
Building values and beliefs	**Confirming**	**Testing**	Drawing together Setting boundaries Creating confidence

One helpful way of looking at questioning is as a constant interaction with understanding. Questions by the coach should open understanding by the learner, who will frequently then be stimulated to ask further questions. The coach has to decide whether those questions are best answered by the learner him- or herself (making the learner dig deeper) or with further contextual information that enables the learner to ask a better question. *The ultimate test of quality for the coach's questioning is the quality of the resulting questions raised by the learner.* This truism is central to the notion of genuine 'learner-centred coaching': it becomes an empowering activity only when the learner him- or herself takes some or all of the responsibility for managing the questioning process.

Observation of coaches at work suggests that when they are truly responsive and sensitive to the learner's evolving understanding, they follow a distinct pattern or cycle of questioning (see Figure 6).

The cycle of questions can be entered or left at any point, but it provides a logical framework by which the coach can ensure that the learner both gains appropriate understanding and uses it to develop realistic plans of action. Challenging questions, as we have seen above, are about causing the learner to take stock and reassess what he or she may have taken for granted. They are often discomforting. An example might be: 'How much of the problem you are having with your colleague could be the result of your own behaviour?'

Probing questions dig deep into the logic and structure of problems, generate alternative ways of looking at things, and suggest new possibilities. For example: 'What behaviours in you might stimulate a different reaction from your colleague?'

Testing questions aim to examine proposed solutions in order to establish whether they are really practical and appropriate. For example: 'So how do you think he would react if you asked for his advice at the beginning of the project rather than half-way through?' Or: 'What are the potential benefits and risks of this approach?'

Confirming questions ensure that coach and learner both have the same understanding of the issue and the options for tackling it – or that they are clear where they do not agree. They often sound like statements: 'So, we've agreed that this is probably a case of behaviour breeds behaviour, and that you could break the negative cycle?'

Challenging and being a critical friend

Recent doctoral research by Jim Butler, director of training and development at Rolls-Royce plc, involved getting people to record what they intended to say in difficult meetings *versus* what they did say and what they thought at the time. Butler concludes that managers fluff an awful lot of learning opportunities because they are not aware of material benefits in challenging what others say or do.

Constructive challenge is one of the most powerful gifts a coach can give to a learner. Challenge can be particularly valuable when it:

☐ makes learners question assumptions and beliefs about themselves or others, or about how the organisation really works

☐ obliges people to test what they do against the values they claim to hold

☐ jolts learners out of sloppy thinking or makes them reconsider half-thought-through solutions

☐ enables learners to consider an issue from an alternative

perspective (even if they then decide that they were right)
☐ stimulates a learning dialogue that would not otherwise
have taken place, and that opens learners' horizons.

Closely allied to constructive challenge is the skill of being a
critical friend – someone who can and will tell you things no
one else will. To become a critical friend, the coach must first
gain the learner's confidence and trust, both in his or her
intentions and in the quality of feedback. When a line manager finds that he or she cannot fulfil this criterion for an individual, then it is important that the manager helps the learner
establish a relationship with an alternative coach, or with an
off-line mentor, whom the learner will trust.

The art of managing challenge can be described as a bal-
ancing-act between challenging and supporting on the one
hand and between empathy and objectivity on the other (see
Figure 7). *Objective challenge* involves giving learners direct
feedback about issues and behaviours of which they may not
be aware, or do not want to be aware. The critical friend role
belongs firmly in this area. *Empathetic challenge* is about
stretching learners' horizons: giving them the encouragement
needed to believe in themselves and their own capabilities.
Empathetic support is needed when learners encounter those
inevitable periods when progress is slow or when they seem
to be getting worse. The effective coach recognises the signs
and is able to reassure the learner that such troughs are a
natural and essential part of achieving a new platform for
development and that a breakthrough will occur. *Objective*

Figure 7
MANAGING CHALLENGE

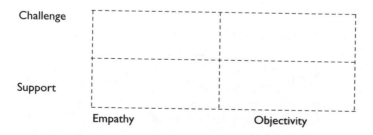

Challenge

Support

Empathy   Objectivity

support is about taking a pragmatic stance, helping the learner to find practical solutions to problems without getting enmeshed in the emotional undergrowth.

Four coaching styles

The style that coaches adopt (according to situation if they are adept, or according to the approach that feels most comfortable to them if they are less competent) appears to depend on two dimensions. The directive–indirective dimension echoes the primary model of 'helping to learn' styles described in brief in Chapter 1. This concerns the question of who is in charge of the relationship and its processes. Who sets the learning goals? Who sets the pace? Who suggests the learning tasks or experiments? Who owns the feedback? The noticeable shift in recent years by writers on coaching towards non-directive behaviours on the part of the coach is admirable, but may sometimes obscure the complexity of the relationship. In practice, the effective coach will vary the directiveness of his or her approach according to the attitudes and behaviour of the learner, moving up and down the learning continuum of 'tell – show – suggest – work it out yourself' by being sensitive to the learner's mood and capability at the time. Although the intensity and durability of learning may be strongest at the 'work it out yourself' end of the spectrum, it may sometimes be necessary to start at a more directive point in order to help the learner gain the confidence to be more proactive.

The second dimension is the intrinsic–extrinsic perspective referred to earlier. The intrinsic perspective focuses attention on the learner and what is happening within him or her: what he or she thinks and feels. The extrinsic perspective looks outwards to how other people see the learner and how other people perform the same tasks. The combination of these dimensions gives rise to four distinct coaching styles, which we can call ASSESSOR, TUTOR, DEMONSTRATOR and STIMULATOR.

Assessors set task and learning goals for the individual. They give feedback based on performance criteria that should be understood by both parties. At the extreme, they rely substantially on telling individuals what is expected, how they

Figure 8
COACHING STYLES

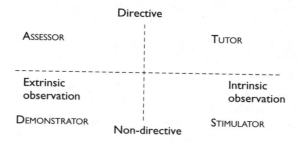

Directive

ASSESSOR   TUTOR

Extrinsic   Intrinsic
observation   observation

DEMONSTRATOR   STIMULATOR

Non-directive

have performed against the expectation, and what they need to do next to improve. This style inevitably takes the ownership of the learning away from learners and, again at the extreme, results in relatively narrow learning: employees learn only what they need to keep the manager off their back! This style sits broadly at the 'tell' end of the coaching spectrum.

Demonstrators are most comfortable at the 'show' stage of the coaching spectrum. They propose learning goals, but allow the individual to decide which to pursue. They show the learner what could be achieved, either by doing it themselves or by reference to other people's experience. The emphasis on showing implies a 'right' way of doing things, but learners are encouraged to adapt what they have seen and to experiment with their own approaches. At their most effective they avoid phrases like 'Do it this way' in favour of more inclusive wording, such as 'What did you notice about the way I dealt with those side issues at the meeting?' or 'Tell me what you observed about how I dealt with that customer's objections.' In doing so, they invite the learner to take partial control of the process.

Effective demonstrators do not just rely on themselves to show how things are done. They create opportunities for the learner to observe other people in action, both good and bad, and then work with the learner through what he or she observed. If the learner cannot work out what he or she should be looking for, or cannot see it, the demonstrator may be obliged to move temporarily to a more directive, tutor style.

Tutors set learning goals but negotiate with the learner about how to achieve them. They typically tell the learner what to observe intrinsically. 'This time, when you jump, think about the position of your trailing leg. How tense are the calf muscles?' Or: 'When you give this speech, think about the degree of eye contact you achieve with the audience.' The tutor/coach draws on his or her own experience to help the learner focus on specific elements of the learning task, and to recognise what he or she should be extracting from each experience. The problem with this style is that by directing the learner's attention towards some observations, the tutor may cause them to tune out other, equally useful observations. Nonetheless, in my own experience of being coached, I have often found it very useful to be given initial pointers in this way. Once I have learned to make the suggested observations, however, and can tell the coach immediately where it felt right and wrong (and her extrinsic observations match my intrinsic ones), it is important to move on and experiment to find other observations of my own that will increase my sensitivity to what is happening. This style corresponds reasonably well with the 'suggest' stage of the coaching spectrum.

Stimulators work with the learner's own goals. They operate at the 'work it out yourself' end of the coaching spectrum, encouraging the learner to apply his or her own logic and experience to the situation. They make extensive use of questions, primarily to maintain the learner's flow of introspective thought – the style can be compared to a light touch on the rudder, making use of the wind and currents already there. This style is much more demanding of the learner, who takes considerable responsibility for the process and needs a certain maturity to cope with uncertainty about where the process is going. The more explorative the dialogue between coach and learner, the greater the potential for both discomfort and discovery!

The key to style management is that it responds directly to the learner's situation and needs as they evolve. The most common reason that managers make poor coaches is that they operate at the same point in the style spectrum whatever the situation. Being stuck in the stimulator style is as bad as being a permanent assessor.

Figure 9
WHAT IS THE LEARNER'S STARTING-POINT?

Experienced coaches choose their style – often instinctively – to match the learner's starting-point. A simple tool for thinking about this is the motivation/ability matrix shown in Figure 9.

In a low-ability, low-motivation situation, the coach will probably have to rely to a considerable amount on 'tell', not least because the person is probably looking for leadership, guidance and a sense of security. The assessor style fits reasonably well here. When a learner has high motivation but low ability, the coach needs to spend more time helping the learner understand the business and sustaining motivation when practical experience knocks him or her back. In this case, a combination of 'tell' and 'suggest' may often be most appropriate. This may best match the demonstrator style. Faced with high ability and low motivation, the coach will need to work hardest on developing motivation and on building confidence: a tutor style. The emphasis will be largely on 'suggest', with an occasional challenge to goad the learner on. Finally, people with high motivation and high ability will usually respond best to a 'work it out for yourself' or stimulator style.

Stepping in and stepping out

One of the most useful techniques for a coach to apply is stepping in and stepping out. Stepping in is about helping the learner with intrinsic observation and reflection; stepping out about helping the learner take an external perspective, looking in at him- or herself and his or her situation.

A typical sequence of coaching questions might look like this:

Stepping in   What happened? (What *really* happened?)

Stepping out   Can you look at it from another perspective?

Stepping in   What do you want to achieve?
                What would that mean for you? For others?

Stepping out   What prevents you?
                What would you advise someone else to do
                in the same position?

Stepping in   How would that work for you?
                How does it feel?

Stepping out   When and how are you going to put it into
                practice?
                What support do you need?

With practice, stepping in and stepping out become instinctive, almost balletic, movements in the learning dialogue. They permit a constant shifting of perspectives that allow both coach and learner to understand more clearly what the issues are and how best to tackle them.

Conclusion

So much of the literature and advice on coaching focuses on what the coach does rather on what he or she enables the learner to do for him- or herself. In the model outlined in this chapter, coaching is a dynamic, learner-centred process in which the coach constantly revises the style of help to meet the learner's circumstances and needs. This does not mean that coaching is a 'soft and cuddling' activity, however. A large part of the role involves encouraging individuals to seek and accept greater and greater challenges – and sometimes placing them in situations where they have to learn how to cope. From this perspective coaching becomes a process of constant stretching – a continuing collusion between coach and learner to reshape the boundaries of achievement.

End-notes

1 ZEMKE R. 'The corporate coach', *Training*, December 1996.
2 GOLEMAN D. *Emotional Intelligence.* London, Bloomsbury, 1996.
PINKER S. *How the Mind Works*, US Norton, 1997/London, Penguin, 1998.

3　THE GUARDIAN

The role of the guardian

When asked to describe people who have been significant in their learning, managers and other employees typically recall a variety of characters, from the 'Worst boss ever – I've used him as a role model of how not to behave ever since' to the very positive 'She gave me a great deal of her time – far more than I thought I deserved.' Ask people in addition to think about those who have significantly influenced their career, and a different cast list may unfold. For a start, far fewer people will have experienced a specific intervention in their career management. And the characters who have steered their careers may not also have provided much in the way of direct transfer of learning.

It is a distinction that has particular significance in another helping role: mentoring. Most of the US literature, and some of the UK and European literature, portrays the mentor as some kind of godfather figure, stepping in from time to time to create opportunities and sponsor the progress of a chosen protégé. The emphasis of the relationship (and it may be a one-way influence) is on developing the individual's career. By contrast, the European perception of mentoring is about developing the individual: the learner takes responsibility for developing his or her own career. The sponsor or godfather is, in effect, an extreme version of the guardian.

The role of guardian can be highly beneficial to all key stakeholders in the relationship – the learner, the guardian and the business – but it is also the most easily abused. The degree to which it is beneficial depends on two factors:

- how (relatively) empowering it is
- how the guardian seeks and achieves reward for his or her efforts.

The empowering guardian

The critical question here is one of dependency v counter-dependency: to what extent does the guardian take control of the objectives and/or the processes of the relationship? One of the most common statements I hear from managers who want to play a helping role towards less experienced people is 'I want to stop them from making the same mistakes I did.' Although this may from time to time be a very practical approach – for example, when the learner is about to make an error that will badly damage his or her career prospects or relationships with key people in the business, or to carry out some action that is illegal, unethical or seriously unprofessional – in general, it is a very arrogant and disempowering attitude. Research by Michael Pearn[1] and colleagues suggests that making mistakes is a critical part of learning. 'Most people never really start to listen to their horse until they've fallen off a few times,' says my riding instructor – and the same principle applies to any activity, from motor skills to management. Mistakes are the most common trigger for self-examination and reflection – the primary fuel for learning. Mix mistakes with the oxygen of reflective dialogue and the spark of insight and you create the explosion of energy that characterises significant learning.

In seeking to prevent the learner from making mistakes, the guardian is acting *in loco parentis* – as a protective parent – rather than as a facilitator of learning who encourages a certain amount of controlled risk-taking. The inevitable result is that the guardian increases his or her own control at the expense of the learner's. In many cases this is unconsciously exactly what he or she wanted to achieve. It can greatly boost a guardian's self-esteem to know that he or she has 'just helped Susan avoid a great disaster' (white knight to the rescue). Equally, it can be highly gratifying for the guardian to assume the mantle of guru, dispensing wisdom from a higher plane of experience (the philosopher holding court), or to exercise his or her influence on behalf of the learner – either with or without the learner's knowledge (the good fairy, or the kingmaker, according to preference).

All of these behaviours must be managed with great care, however, because they can all too easily become focused on satisfying the guardian's needs more than the learner's. The effective guardian is constantly questioning his or her own motivations and asking not 'What can I do for the learner?'

but 'What can I help the learner to do for himself or herself?'

A great deal more could be said about power in helping relationships, but we have more pressing issues to move on to. Appendix 1 pulls together some additional strands for those who wish to pursue this theme further.

How the guardian seeks reward for his or her efforts

The effective, empowering guardian does not look for self-gratification through boosting his or her own sense of importance or self-worth. Rather, he or she sees the relationship as a valuable source of learning for both parties. It is a social exchange: experience, wisdom and (if and where appropriate) an exercise of influence in exchange for freshness of approach, candid questioning and challenge from someone less normalised into the system. This requires an emotional maturity in the guardian sufficient to overcome the natural *gravitas* of position and authority. Most of the effective guardians I have encountered over the years have a fairly strong capacity for poking fun at themselves and for willingly accepting good-humoured attempts to puncture any tendency they may have towards pomposity. Another common characteristic of effective guardians is that although they may receive gratitude for their efforts on the learner's behalf, they very rarely expect or demand it. On the contrary, they often express gratitude themselves for having been allowed to share in the younger person's development.

What does frequently turn them on is their reputation as a developer of people. Particularly at middle-management levels, where personal career plateauing is a fact of business life, the manager can feel that he or she is making an increased contribution, over and above task delivery, in terms of bringing out and developing talent. The more this is recognised by the organisation, the more of an incentive this becomes. The ability to spot, nurture and release talent into the organisation is one of the most valuable skills a manager can acquire.

Four styles of guardian

As in each of the other core helping roles, the guardian can operate within a variety of relationship styles. Once again, a

Figure 10
GUARDIAN STYLES

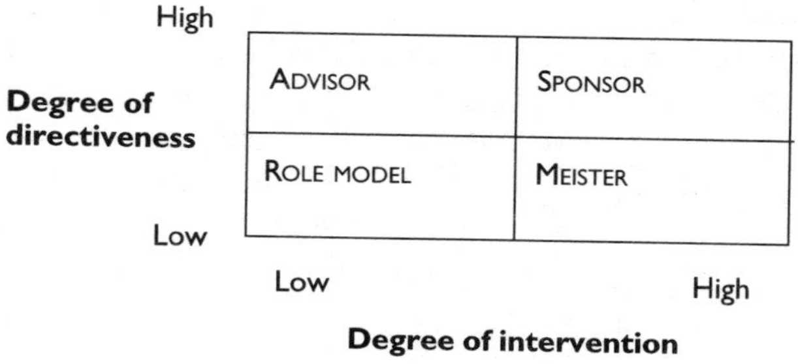

High

**Degree of
directiveness**

ADVISOR	SPONSOR
ROLE MODEL	MEISTER

Low

Low   High

Degree of intervention

defining axis of the relationship style is directive v non-directive (the latter being relative, because the guardian style, like coaching, will almost always be to some extent directive). The other axis, however, is the degree of intervention that the guardian exercises.

The resulting four styles can be described as:

- role model
- advisor
- meister
- sponsor.

Role model

In practice, anyone engaging in one-on-one learning relationships will be something of a role model. Consciously or unconsciously, along with the transfer of knowledge there will be a transfer of behaviours, ways of thinking, and mental models of how the organisation and its environment work. However, in the guardian role the tendency for the learner to emulate is particularly high, for a number of reasons.

Firstly, the reason people come together into this kind of relationship is typically because they see something special in each other. The guardian is either reminded by someone of him- or herself at the same career stage or sees someone who has potential that could be developed by example. The learner may see someone who has succeeded in the areas where he or she too has aspirations and who represents who and what he or she wants to be. (Research by Gill Lane[2] suggests, however, that the greatest attraction for the learner is the mentor's behavioural competence.)

Secondly, the learner often enters into this kind of relationship out of vulnerability, either recognised by him- or herself or by the guardian. (If you are feeling vulnerable yourself, it can be comforting to build a relationship with someone even more vulnerable.) The more vulnerable you feel, the more likely you are to seek role models in other people rather than develop your own vision of what you want to become.

A third, contrasting reason is that many people seek a relationship with a guardian not out of vulnerability but out of ambition. They want a powerful figure whose influence can help them achieve personal objectives faster than they would on their own. Having a successful role model to copy is a useful means of speeding up progress towards the learner's goals.

I had a powerful illustration recently of the potential of role models to have an influence for good or ill in a UK company that had bungled the line placements of a group of graduate recruits during their two-year induction. Instead of placing them with good role models the company had simply pushed them into any slot that was available. Those who had had good role models were perceived as having potential; the others were seen as problem children. Given a different environment and a better role model, however, the senior managers' views of the problem children changed rapidly as the graduates showed what they could do. What had been observed was not the true capabilities of the graduates but the reflected behaviours of their supervising line managers. It could be argued that all young potential managers should be given a number of role models to match themselves against, to guard against being overly influenced by one poor one.

As this example illustrates, quality of role model provided is an important ingredient in the nature and value of the learning that takes place. But how do you define quality? Because each learner has a different set of needs and potential, a good role model for me might not be a good role model for you. Take the example of a would-be sales manager who used his boss – a very successful salesman – as his role model. The boss spent almost all of his time on the road, working with the field staff and joining in on the big pitches. It worked so well for him that the company tolerated the near-chaos of the paperwork, which he tackled only when he had to. By the time the learner received his own territory and sales team, he had learned to operate in much the same way – but he did not have the personality to jolly people along as easily, and the stresses on his home life that resulted from constantly being away began to tell on his health. Only by stepping back and re-examining what he wanted to be and what he regarded as success did he recognise that he had been following what was for him a false model. He actually enjoyed organising and directing and was good at it. He cut down his time in the field to more manageable proportions and got the sales team to come to him, in small groups, where they could learn from each other. And he focused his time on activities that supported them. Before long he was outperforming his old boss, and eventually became his manager. The original boss/role model eventually went elsewhere, complaining how the company had 'just got too bureaucratic'.

Even if you select the 'right' role models, they are not going to be perfect. Everyone has flaws, even if they are not immediately obvious. Moreover, the strengths people have – those aspects that others are most likely to emulate – may also be their greatest weaknesses if used inappropriately or to excess. The brilliant public speaker who never gets off his platform, the person with superb eye for detail who never sees the big picture, the manager who always achieves the task yet often fails to count the cost – these are all common characters from whom we can learn both positively and negatively.

For effective role modelling to take place, both parties must be realistic about what behaviours and mental models are to be transferred. An exercise that I often use with managers is to ask them to list three things that other people could usefully use them as a role model for, and three things that it would be disastrous for others to copy. The same data from other people who know them well is also useful input to understanding where it would be helpful to discuss with the learner how he or she is going to manage the largely osmotic process of learning by role modelling.

One outcome of these discussions between learner and helper is often that the learner receives much more thoughtful advice on the areas in which the guardian acknowledges a weakness than he or she would from someone for whom it is a natural strength. If you are aware of a weakness, have thought about it a great deal, and have struggled to overcome it, you are much more likely to have useful mental models to convey than someone who just 'does it'. You will have far more empathy with someone who is also struggling with that issue. The guardian in such cases may well find him- or herself operating in a coaching manner.

Another common outcome is that the learner gains greater insight into other negative role models and how to use them. In getting people to talk about their learning experiences, I often encourage them to recollect powerful examples of negative learning – times when they have observed behaviour by others and determined never to be like that. The more conscious people are of what is and what is not 'good' behaviour, the more studiously they will attempt to avoid being like the negative role model.

Equally, the more they are able to identify those aspects of the negative role model's behaviour which they *should* emulate. For example, I once had as a boss an appallingly bad people manager who I often use as a negative yardstick for my own behaviour, so powerful an impact did he have on me and everyone else who worked for him. But that manager had a code of ethics with regard to the integrity of the work that was far more stringent than that of any other publisher in Europe. It became a source of pride that whereas other periodicals would happily accept free trips to visit companies abroad, this one would insist on paying its own costs, so it could never be accused of being influenced in the stories it wrote. It never occurred to me until years later that I had adapted and applied those same ethics to a whole variety of business decisions, and that this had become a strength for me too.

Bringing such issues to the surface to develop a realistic and pragmatic approach to role modelling is much more difficult when it happens without the conscious involvement of one or both parties. Time and again people describe some of their most influential learning experiences in terms that suggest that the role models were entirely unaware they were the object of such regard. Why did they not make the relationship overt? Typically through embarrassment or lack of courage to approach the person. When they do make the relationship overt it may be through the intervention of a third party – a coach, counsellor, mentor or facilitator, or simply a good friend.

Sometimes people prefer to observe and model from afar, never making meaningful contact at all. There is nothing substantially wrong with doing so, of course, but it does mean that the learner never has the opportunity to dig beneath the surface. Copying the behaviour without understanding the thinking can be very dangerous. For example, a CEO found that he sometimes needed to make a dramatic gesture to demonstrate how important an issue was. So he occasionally pretended to lose his temper, banging the table and shouting to make the point. Observing this behaviour, some junior managers adopted a similar style in dealing with their direct reports. However, they lacked his instinctive understanding of when to use such drastic measures. By losing their temper frequently, they not only alienated their direct reports, they ensured that people very rarely took their tantrums seriously.

Organisations need to recognise the value of such relationships and encourage people to speak up when they identify a role model or when they feel a role model would be useful and would like suggestions of where to look. Although role modelling goes on all the time in organisations, it has been inadequately sold and deserves a much better press.

A good example of simple but effective use of planned role modelling is the 'If I can, you can' scheme run by the Fair Play for Women organisation. The scheme brings successful career women into schools to discuss their experience and provide support for girls. Providing role models in such areas as entrepreneurship or engineering opens up wider horizons for both girls and boys: some boys gain the confidence to opt for atypical careers such as nursing.

Figure 11
EVOLUTION OF ROLE MODEL RELATIONSHIPS

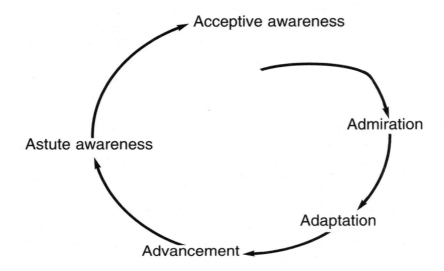

How people learn to outgrow their role models

Relationships with role models typically evolve through stages that are relatively clearly discernible. Mature individuals will often have undergone several cycles of role modelling, each time becoming wiser in the way they approach the learning potential of the situation. In effect, they turn the cycle into a spiral (see Figure 11). Less mature individuals may find it hard to move on within the cycle and so may enter into a series of role modelling relationships, abandoning each in turn as it fails to deliver.

The key stages are:

☐ *acceptive awareness* – identifying from a distance someone who represents the values or achievements you identify with. The learner 'sees something' in this individual that sets him or her out from the crowd, and feels that this person may have something to teach. As a young journalist I developed an acceptive awareness of Peter Drucker as someone whose achievements I would like to emulate. I never took the next step of seeking Drucker out. However,

I did develop a friendship with consultant John Humble (of Management by Objectives fame), who had very specifically used Drucker as a role model.

- *admiration* – moving from the general to the specific as a result of personal interaction or direct observation of the role model. The more the learner hears of the role model's values, ideas and approaches, the deeper the admiration. The learner begins consciously to compare him- or herself against what he or she observes (or believes to observe – it is all too easy to see through rose-tinted glasses) and to identify areas for personal improvement or goals for personal achievement.

- *adaptation* – consciously or unconsciously (or both) attempting to adopt the role model's *Weltanschauung* [world-philosophy], behaviour or values. At this stage, the learner may do so fairly uncritically, both because of feeling so inadequate in comparison to the role model and because of feeling empowered by an embodiment of what he or she too could become.

- *advancement* – True learning begins when the learner exerts his or her critical faculties and begins to integrate the role model's mental models with his or her own, rather than simply accepting them 'as is'.

- *astute awareness* – This is when the scales fall from the learner's eyes, and he or she sees the role model more clearly, recognising the latter's frailty and humanness as important parts of the whole individual. The learner evaluates what the role model represents and decides which aspects to absorb into and which to reject from his or her own views and behaviours. The learner may use this new-found knowledge to seek out new role models but will begin with a much clearer perception of what he or she can and should absorb this time around, drawing on his or her own underlying values and beliefs.

Exactly what people choose – consciously or unconsciously – to emulate in their role models will obviously vary greatly from individual to individual. But a recent study by Gill Lane[3] suggests that the emphasis of this subtle transfer of behaviours is typically greater on personal development than on either career issues or issues in their current work role.

Advisor

The areas people seek advice on in the workplace are very diverse. Yet some are sufficiently common and important enough to warrant specific comment. In particular:

□ *'how things work here'* – The systems, structures and (perhaps most important of all, in career terms) the politics of the organisation; the newer the learner is to the organisation, the greater is his or her need for advice on how to achieve social fit, how to get around the formal systems and procedures to get things done, and how to forge useful alliances.

□ *interpersonal issues* – From how to deal with a difficult boss, to how to motivate a team.

□ *handling a radically different situation* – What should I do on Day One in a new job to make the right impression?

□ *career self-management* – How should I evaluate the choices available to me? How do people get on in this organisation? Where can I find a mentor?

Advising on any of these topics may rapidly lead into taking on another helping role – that of coach, career-counsellor or networker. In doing so, the helper shifts the ownership of issue back towards the learner. Simply giving advice ensures that the ownership stays with the guardian.

Giving advice is such a natural part of day-to-day activity that it is undervalued. Yet advice-giving is often a profession of high value – witness the salaries and bonuses of such knowledge workers as solicitors, IT consultants and Harley Street specialist doctors. In all these examples the quality of the advice is important in setting the price – quality reckoned as a mixture of factors, including depth and/or breadth of relevant experience, standard of judgement, peer reputation and the level of consideration the advisor gives to the client's issue.

The same principles apply, if with less force, to the way managers and experienced employees give advice to others. To be truly helpful, it has to be done in a thoughtful and considered manner rather than off the cuff. It has to be as unbiased as possible, separated from any of the advisor's own agendas. How the learner values the advice will depend to a considerable extent on the level of respect the learner has for the advisor, in terms of his or her integrity, perspicacity and track record of good judgement in other, similar situations. In short, people grow into the role of advisor as their own wisdom grows.

The dangers of giving unsolicited advice are obvious. It is more likely to be resented and rejected. And it is heavily disempowering. Yet sometimes it is essential to take people aside and explain to them the impact and consequences of their behaviour, for their own protection. The guardian needs to exercise considerable discretion in working across a spectrum that looks something like Table 3.

Table 3
A SPECTRUM OF DIRECTIVENESS

Directive			Non-directive
Tell them what they need to know	Ask if they would welcome advice in a specific area	Suggest issues to explore together, where they can decide when to seek advice	Encourage them generally to seek advice; educate in how to recognise when they need advice

Before moving to the directive end of the spectrum, the effective advisor will:

- identify precisely what the issue is
- establish what thinking-through the learner has already done – how would he or she advise someone else in a similar situation?
- establish where else the learner has sought advice on this topic, if at all, and how he or she feels about the advice given
- check that the learner really *does* want advice, rather than an opportunity to think matters through for him- or herself
- consider how the advice should best be delivered – as a set of options, as a general background, or as specific recommendations.

All too often managers simply jump in at the final stage, responding to a request for advice with an opinion: 'I suggest you . . .', 'If you want to get the best out of that team, you will need to . . .', 'There are three key things you'll have to watch out for in dealing with this kind of project . . .'. As a result, the learner may feel that the advisor lacks real interest in, and understanding of, the learner's issues, and that the advice given is general, rather than specific. At the same time, however, the manager who constantly holds back from giving advice when a simple word here and there would be welcome and helpful is at best irritating and likely to be highly damaging to the learner's confidence. The exercise of judgement is, once again, a key skill.

Meister

At one level, the *meister* is the proactive *doppelgänger* of the role model. He or she is very, very good at the job, and gathers together a coterie of (usually) younger people with whom he or she shares experience and confidences. The *meister* demands and receives exceptional loyalty and, in extreme cases this may extend to an unwritten rule that his or her opinions are not to be questioned or challenged. Often very astute at identifying talent, the *meister* may either cause it to blossom – by providing opportunities to participate at a different, higher level – or may stifle it, as the mature oak overshadows all younger competition.

Meisters can be remarkably effective at attracting and rapidly developing raw talent. But they can also be very impatient and dismissive of those who do not fit the mould. For the learner, association with a *meister* can be a stimulating, exhilarating experience, a roller-coaster of exposure to challenge after challenge. But the price to pay in terms of independence and choosing one's own paths to learning may be too great for many people and therefore counter-productive to learning in the longer run.

Sponsor

In the American best-selling book and film *The Firm* Gene Hackman plays the part of a wise and experienced figure who shows a young attorney the ropes. Given that the firm is run by the Mafia, it might have been more appropriate to refer to Hackman's character as a godfather, but he is never important enough. He is, however, sufficiently important to promote the younger person's career, to intervene to protect him from time to time, and *to use his influence to do things on the younger person's behalf*. Similarly, in the film *The Godfather* the eponymous character dispenses favours and makes career breaks happen for people under his protection, notably the Sinatra-like crooner.

Because of their power and influence, sponsors can and do make offers people cannot refuse, unless they choose to work elsewhere. But they can also open doors – lots of them. Effective sponsors take it on themselves to:

- identify posts and projects that will give the learner high visibility and a high degree of challenge
- put the learner forward for those opportunities and make his or her case where it counts
- shield the learner from the worst effects of mistakes or misalliances he or she has made
- introduce the learner to the 'right' clubs – those peopled by other movers and shakers with the gift of learning opportunities and promotion.

It is not a style that fits easily with current-day views of equal opportunity and self-sufficiency. On the contrary, informal sponsorship will almost always lead to élitism and cloning, minorities and others from the wrong background getting short shrift. Yet sponsorship can be a very powerful means of overcoming these same problems. Giving people from disadvantaged groups a sponsor in the organisation can ensure that they *do* get more equal access to learning opportunities. The trade-off is that their achievements will not be entirely due to their own efforts.

Managing guardian styles

When any of these styles is allowed to go to the extreme, the potential for abuse increases rapidly. If too much stress is placed on the role model and advisor styles, a guru–acolyte relationship can rapidly develop. Too much emphasis on the sponsor style looks dangerously like a godfather role. Hyperactive *meisters* can develop a circle of overdependent 'gofers'.

Where the guardian role is played with the learner's consent and compliance, there is a real danger, in many cases, of developing overdependency on one or both sides.

A study of mentoring in the USA some years ago[4] that focused primarily on guardian–protégé type relationships found that a very high proportion of relationships ended in tears, one side forcing the other out of the organisation. This is not surprising when we consider how disempowering the guardian role can be if it is not thoughtfully applied. No matter how well appreciated the attentions of the more powerful person may be originally, unless the guardian knows how and when to back off as the learner becomes more confident and competent, the learner will eventually begin to resent the relationship. Very often, the stronger the original dependency, the stronger the subsequent counterdependency (the determination not to be beholden to the guardian). Anyone who has had teenage children will be familiar with the emotional cauldron this process evokes.

Where the guardian role is played without the learner's consent and compliance, the effect can be very negative. I have on a number of occasions encountered young graduates who have quit firms because they did not welcome the attentions – however well meant – of a senior player. In some cases the senior persons were attempting – although they probably did not recognise it as such – to relive their own careers through someone else. What they failed to recognise was that the younger persons had their own ideas about their career choices and wanted to do things for themselves. (It isn't only young people that suffer from this phenomenon: anybody more junior can find themselves at the mercy of unwelcome advice!)

All of this sounds very negative, but in reality the guardian role, when well-managed, has the potential to give the learner a great deal of relevant and timely support. The keys to managing it effectively are:

☐ Remember that it is the learner's interests that come first, and that he or she has to define what those interests are.

☐ Draw down, not pour down – the guardian should emphasise reactive, responsive rather than proactive, 'taking
charge' behaviour.

☐ Recognise the link between other 'helping to learn roles' –
for a guardian to identify a valuable development opportunity opens up potential for further support via coaching,
and possibly also via networking and counselling.

☐ Seek to empower the learner whenever possible – even if
this means starting off in a directive manner and gradually
encouraging him or her to take more ownership of the
process.

☐ Recognise the limitations of what you can and should do
on behalf of the learner.

Conclusion

Guardianship is arguably the most complex of development
alliance roles. The power to shape other people's views,
behaviours and careers can be highly seductive, especially if
the learner becomes like oneself. The potential to disem-
power is vast, especially where the guardian falls into the trap
of becoming a father-substitute.

Yet at the same time the guardian role can be truly liberating,
providing learners with an enhanced vision of their own potential, opening their eyes to new opportunities and helping them
develop their own paths through the corporate minefield.

The key lies in the attitudes of the helper and the learner –
the degree to which the latter is prepared to sacrifice independence for security and the former to focus on the learner's
needs rather than his or her own. If the relationship is to fulfil
its development potential, a degree of personal maturity and
self-sacrifice is essential in the guardian, whereas the learner
needs to exercise discretion and a certain amount of healthy
scepticism about how he or she perceives the guardian and
how much he or she really wants to be like that person.

End-notes

1 Pearn M., Mulrooney C. and Payne T. *Learning from
Mistakes: How individuals and organisations need to learn.*

2 LANE G. *and* ROBINSON A. 'Assessing work-based learning', *Manager Update*, vol. 4 no. 1, 1992.
3 LANE G. 'Competences of mentors', doctoral thesis, 1997.
4 LEE M. 'Playing the guru: inequality of personal power in relationships', *Management Education and Development*, vol. 22 pt 4, 1991.

4   THE WORKPLACE
COUNSELLOR

Defining and describing a counsellor

Counselling has come in for a remarkably bad press in recent years. As with coaching and mentoring, almost anyone can set up in business as a paid counsellor, guiding people through difficult personal decisions. But the consequences of getting counselling wrong, or providing poor counselling, are often much greater than with any other form of helping people. Paid counsellors have been blamed for poor career decisions, false memory syndrome and a variety of other ills. The more serious the issues the learner faces, the greater the potential for getting it wrong.

It does not help, either, that the term 'counselling' has such a diversity of meanings. Among the most common are:

- a therapist/psychoanalyst, helping the individual identify and deal with issues that affect his or her unconscious behaviour and personality
- a consultant, as in 'small-business counsellor' (it is unfortunate that many small-business advisors have recently started to refer to themselves as business mentors – a role for which they are rarely qualified)
- a specialist advisor, as in 'career counsellor'
- a lawyer, in American English, or a local politician, in British English (the spelling may be different but the derivation is the same)
- a tutor, with pastoral responsibility for his or her charges.

For our purposes, in the role of helping a learner, counselling is an essential part of the helper's toolkit. It encompasses a range of behaviours and skills, including:

- helping people develop the confidence and motivation to tackle a learning task/seize a learning opportunity

- helping them towards insight into their own drives and fears so that they can recognise and accept the need for improvement or change
- helping them plan what and how they will change about themselves (ie how they will learn)
- helping them develop coping strategies to overcome barriers to achievement and to learning
- being available to offer support, or simply to listen sympathetically, when needed
- acting as a gateway to other forms of professional help – eg legal, medical, or psychotherapeutic, where the learner has specific needs beyond the counsellor's competence.

The last bullet point is one of the most critical. As with all the helping roles covered in this book, a fundamental skill is knowing where the boundaries of the role, and one's own competence to help, lie. Many, if not most, of the problems associated with counselling appear to arise because the counsellor is drawn into areas that he or she lacks the training or skills to tackle. The line manager who takes on a direct report's marriage problems, for example, is almost certainly stepping beyond the legitimate role of day-to-day counselling at work. Perhaps the most dangerous person in the organisation is the one who is unaware of his or her limitations in offering counsel and/or who assumes the possession of skills that are in fact missing.

In our work with senior executives at CPS, the evaluation of potential mentors by a specialist assessor has been invaluable in pointing up a particularly dangerous kind of would-be helper-of-others. This character, drawn to the pseudo-psychological by his or her own need to be understood, has often completed a wide spectrum of psychometric tests but has never internalised the lessons from them. This person's need to become involved in the problems and issues of others is a substitute for tackling his or her own. To look inwards is too painful: it is far easier and more comfortable to transfer the anxieties to someone else. Such people drift from one neatly packaged behavioural theory or nostrum to another. They never find what they are looking for because they never look in the right place – within themselves.

Most of the established forms of psychotherapy expect practitioners to undergo the same kind of therapy themselves. This is partly so that the practitioner experiences the process and can at least to some extent take the client's perspective. But it is also important for helpers to gain a deep insight into their own drives, motivations and emotional weak spots. To understand others, one must first understand oneself.

Much the same applies to the counselling activities of managers in organisations. To develop the thinking patterns that make for an effective counsellor at work, it helps greatly for the manager to be on the receiving end. From a sheer practical point of view, for example, how can you realistically talk with other people about planning their career for the next five years if you have given no significant thought to your own? It is possible to think your own career plan through in isolation, but, as we have already discussed in the section on personal reflective space (pages 15–16), it will normally be much more beneficial to conduct the dialogue with someone else who can ask questions and see from perspectives you might not.

What is workplace counselling?

The short-list of activities above is about as close to an acceptable definition of counselling at work as I have been able to extract. However, other ways of looking at it may be useful. All forms of helping to learn lie on a spectrum from reactive (where the helper changes as well as the learner) to catalytic (where the helper remains essentially unchanged). Table 4 puts the most common helping styles into this spectrum. Counselling lies near the extreme catalytic end of the spectrum because it requires the helper to maintain a high level of detachment. That detachment is necessary to help learners de-couple from their emotional chains and focus on the issues. However, counselling is not about denying emotion. On the contrary, it is about developing an understanding of emotion, and how the individual's emotions affect his or her perceptions, judgement and behaviour. This is as true for career counselling as it is for counselling someone on a severe behavioural issue. The values that the learner applies and the

Table 4

THE SPECTRUM OF PERSONAL CHANGE

Reagent					Catalyst
Mentor	Coach	Tutor	Networker	Sponsor	Counsellor

feelings that he or she has about different choices are fundamental to the process.

One possible way of defining workplace counselling, therefore, is 'preparing the emotional ground for learning'. There is a massive amount of evidence from research studies to suggest that emotional state and learning performance are inextricably linked. Students who approach their examinations with confidence generally perform better than those who are worried, even when both have similar levels of IQ and have studied equally diligently. Soothing music helps the absorption of information. And people who have clear learning goals typically achieve more learning than those who are unclear about what they need to learn and why.

Part of preparing the emotional ground for learning is clearing away the debris – fears, repetitive behaviours, tunnel vision and other barriers – that prevent the individual from:

☐ recognising a development need

☐ understanding the development need

☐ accepting the validity of the need

☐ deciding to do something about it

☐ planning how to tackle it

☐ maintaining the motivation to achieve personal change.

The role of the counsellor may cover any or all of these issues. Let's look at each in a little more detail.

Recognising a development need

The following is a much-abbreviated version of a counselling session with a public-sector chief executive.

CEO: I'm concerned I can't get people in this organisation to pay more than lip-service to performance management. We've had discussions about it, I've stressed how important it is, but nothing seems to happen.

Counsellor: Why is it so important to you that this particular system is taken seriously?

CEO: Because it's central to our strategic plan. We have to cut costs year on year and we've got to find new ways of using our time efficiently. People will talk about performance management on the steering committees, but not apply it to their own departments.

Counsellor: What are the most critical performance areas for you?

CEO: I hadn't thought about it in those terms ... I could write them down in five minutes if I had to.

Counsellor: Think about what you've just said. What message does that send to other people?

[*Silence, for about 30 seconds*]

CEO: If I'm going to ask other people to change their behaviour radically, I've got to demonstrate that I've done it, too ... If I'm clear about my performance measures and how I'm doing against them, and *they* are too, then I've got a much stronger moral case ...

This scenario, with different issues, is played out time and time again within effective workplace counselling. The problems with others that cause the person stress and worry are all too often at least partly problems within him- or herself – or, at least, can be tackled by a change of perspective and a willingness to take the issue on one's own shoulders rather than continue to off-load it onto other people's. Behavioural learning begins when the person becomes aware that he or she is part of the problem.

Of course, counselling is not the only way in which this recognition stage occurs. The learner may receive feedback from his or her own manager, from peers, or from a variety of other sources that force him or her to re-evaluate. The would-be playwright whose manuscript is rejected with the comment 'Needs much more characterisation' has a vital and helpful clue. What he or she may not have at this stage is a clear understanding of what that means. For that, the best way forward may be to seek advice from someone who does know or who can explore the meaning with him or her. The latter role may require a counselling style to help define the learning need in terms in which it can be tackled. At that point the learner may need the help of a coach, to plan and manage the learning of new skills or behaviours.

Understanding the development need

One of the most common problems with performance appraisals is getting people to understand what is meant by each area of development need. For example, research into communication capability of managers by the ITEM Group found that most organisations which had competence statements included 'communication' as one of the subsets of behaviour people were expected to demonstrate. But definitions of what that meant were almost invariably vague and left a great deal to the imagination of the appraiser and the appraisee. When the research subsequently identified nine clusters of communication situations, five core skills and eight styles of communication, it greatly expanded the vocabulary by which people could discuss their development need.

In many situations, however, the vocabulary does not exist. The learner has to create his or her own vocabulary to explain the situation and the changes needed. An effective counsellor can help the learner develop a picture of where he or she is starting from and where he or she is aiming to be. Taking the communication example again, the learner whose job involves occasional public speaking may need to appreciate how the audience reacts now, how he or she creates that reaction, what reaction he or she wants the audience to have, and what behaviours the learner could exhibit that would give rise to that reaction.

Techniques for putting the learner back into situations in which he or she has felt confident and successful in tackling the work task, and into others in which he or she has felt diffident and unsuccessful, are very useful in achieving this kind of understanding. (If the learner has not experienced the former, then visioning what it would be like is a reasonable substitute.) The more senses the learner can apply in this process (visual, auditory, recalled emotion, and so on), the more powerful his or her recollection is likely to be. In each case the counsellor is, in effect, helping such people to make their own comparisons, to develop their own ways of explaining what they did differently, and to build their own motivation to improve.

Accepting the validity of the need

Knowing that you *could* change is not the same as agreeing that you *should*. Most smokers are aware of the dangers of their habit, but it may take a life-threatening event or the trauma of the death from lung cancer of a close friend or relative to convince them that the dangers apply equally to them. Much the same is true of development needs identified at traditional appraisals: the learner's sign-up may be motivated from a whole range of reasons other than a genuine commitment to change.

Consider it from the appraisee's point of view. If you have just had a positive review, are you really going to spoil the atmosphere by arguing about the smattering of less positive items presented to you by your manager? It is much easier to rationalise the information away on the basis that the manager would lose credibility with his or her superiors if the evaluation did not contain some negatives. Indeed, I have received appraisals where my manager said as much, openly. If you have just received a negative appraisal, your first fear will be about keeping your job. Although you may argue some points, your instincts are likely to be towards compliance, agreeing to address the failings pointed out to you. But compliance and public agreement do not amount to internal acceptance. Indeed, resentment against the overall tone of the appraisal may increase your resistance to those development needs that you would otherwise have accepted from your own self-knowledge. You need to deal with the emotional context before you can deal with the development issues.

Effective counselling can help the learner put these natural feelings aside and focus on the issues and on desirable outcomes. Letting off steam may be an essential first step, before getting down to 'OK, so what are you going to do about it?' Three issues are important here:

1 Managing perception v managing reality. Even if the individual does not accept that there is a problem or weakness

in actual skill or behaviour, he or she can usually be brought to an understanding that certain other key people do not see it the same way. They therefore have an issue (in their mind) of perception management rather than an innate need to change themselves. In practice, it does not matter a great deal because the best way to change negative perceptions is to put even more effort into showing how good you really are. If the change in behaviour elicits positive comment from a wider circle of people, the learner is likely in due course to admit to him- or herself that the original criticism was just after all.

2　'Do I value the opinion of the person making the criticism?' (I am grateful to consultant and professional mentor Rennie Fritchie for raising this and the following question.) The more respect the learner has for the individual who points out the learning need, the more seriously he or she is likely to take it. The workplace counsellor helps the learner explore feelings towards the source of criticism. Does he or she discount their opinion because they have a track record of being wrong in such matters, because there is hostility or rivalry between them and the learner, because the other person is known to be working to a different agenda, and so on? Does he or she accept the opinion because the source is a good friend, a more influential person, and so on? The clearer the learner can be about his or her own motivations in assessing developmental feedback, the easier it will be to accept the need for personal change.

3　'Does that person's opinion matter?' Whether that person is right or wrong, if the person making the criticism has a significant influence over your job or career, it is self-defeating to ignore what is said. If the individual does not ask the question of him- or herself, then the counsellor must ask it.

Deciding to do something about it

Taking the smoking example a little further, even a traumatic event may not be enough to push the smoker from acceptance of need to commitment to do something about it. Similarly, the desks of managers are often littered with tasks that they know need to be done but that never seem to come to the top of the pile. Early research in 'total quality' found that many of the most impactful improvements had been on the books for months or years. Procrastination is an inbuilt human defence against pain and stress, although an accumulation of tasks set aside can result in much greater stress.

One of the most useful tools I have found in helping people examine the depth of their commitment to learning goals is *The meaning of 'yes'*. This very simple tool asks learners to say where they believe themselves to be on the following scale:

Figure 12

THE MEANING OF 'YES'

7	Yes –	... I'll dedicate myself to seeing this through
6	Yes –	... I'm committed to following this up
5	Yes –	... I'm willing to help follow that up
4	Yes –	... There's something in this
3	Yes –	... This is exciting and engaging
2	Yes –	... It's quite interesting
1	Yes –	... I'll go along with it
0	Yes –	... over my dead body

Once learners have assigned a level to their commitment it becomes possible to discuss, where appropriate, how they can raise their commitment or whether they are genuinely content to avoid the issue and/or stay as they are. In the latter case the counsellor may then need to back off. It is not his or her role *as a counsellor* to pressure the individual to change. But the issue may be appropriate for the line manager to tackle, within his or her role as coach.

This raises the question of whether the line manager can legitimately and practically also be the counsellor to his or her direct reports. Unlike the role separation between line management and mentoring (where the two roles are manifestly incompatible, except in the traditional US model), this issue is much less clear. Line managers do need to adopt counselling behaviours from time to time as part of the internal support systems of the well-functioning team. But what if the issues that concern the learner are partly or wholly bound up in the manager's own relationship with the learner? The answer appears to lie, once again, in where the role boundaries are set. The line manager as counsellor is rather like the general practitioner in medicine – qualified to prescribe pills and potions at a certain level but skilled also in recognising when to pass the patient on into other hands. The other hands could be those of an off-line coach or mentor, or of a professional counsellor (for example, a bereavement counsellor), or could be represented by an impersonal gateway, such as an employee advice programme.

Planning how to tackle the need

Commitment to change is not enough. There has to be a process by which the learner proceeds step by step towards the learning or career goal. The development counsellor can help the learner think through how to structure a self-development plan, where to find the support and resources needed and how to take the first steps.

Maintaining the motivation to achieve personal change

By this stage the individual has either taken firm charge of his or her own learning or has secured the help of a coach. Continued motivation often demands positive feedback about progress. The line manager/coach and such other people as peers are obvious sources here. But what if a series of setbacks causes the learner to doubt his or her own ability and begin to lose motivation? It may be necessary to revisit the processes that led to the commitment to change in the first place. Were some of the assumptions and insights wrong? Are the repeated failures actually the result of a fear of succeeding? Whereas the coach may be able to help the learner analyse what happened and why from observation of events, the counsellor may be able to help the learner dig deeper and analyse how his or her beliefs, assumptions and feelings have set him or her up for failure.

Dimensions of counselling

All of the activities we have described so far under the heading of counselling fit neatly into the matrix below. This defines counselling in terms of two critical dimensions:

☐ *coping and growing* – The *purpose* of the helping relationship may be either coping (coming to terms with the working or social environment) or growing (developing personal competence, self-reliance). In practice, most counselling relationships will operate on both axes of this dimension, moving up and down according to the issue and how far the learner has got in tackling it.

☐ *looking out and looking in* –The *perspective* of the relationship may be external (How can I affect/manipulate/master the world around me?) or internal (How can I gain greater insight and mastery over myself?) Again the two perspectives are complementary and an effective counsellor will help the learner move between them – sometimes many times in a single counselling session.

Figure 13
COUNSELLING STYLES

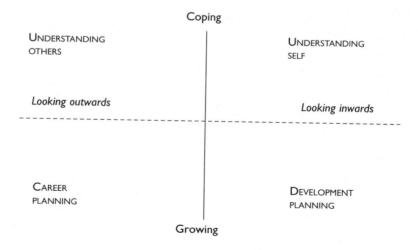

Not surprisingly (if you have read this far), these dimensions give rise to four relatively clear counselling styles: UNDERSTANDING OTHERS, UNDERSTANDING SELF, CAREER PLANNING and DEVELOPMENT PLANNING.

Understanding others: helping the learner gain insight into his or her relationships with others; to identify repetitive cycles of interaction; to become more sensitive to other people's motivations and perspectives; to develop awareness of his or her impact upon other people's behaviour. And to develop strategies for managing relationships more effectively.

Understanding self: helping the learner gain insight into his or her own unconscious processes; to recognise and deal with dysfunctional blindspots that affect his or her social and/or task performance. And to develop strategies for managing themselves more effectively.

Career planning: advising the learner about career choices; helping evaluate and choose between opportunities, develop a strategy and broad plan for career development.

Development planning: helping the learner make use of self-knowledge to develop his or her own resilience, envision what he or she might become, and plan how to get there.

In practice, these four roles are heavily interdependent. It may very often (perhaps always) be essential to help learners understand themselves before they can realistically begin the process of development planning, or to understand others. It is equally difficult to make realistic career plans without an understanding of other people and a development plan – and a healthy self-awareness can be pretty useful, too. Equally, gaining insight into oneself may require the stimulus of a career ambition, an interpersonal problem or a defined development need. The effective workplace counsellor moves from one role to the other with ease to match the learner's need.

The skills of an effective counsellor at work

In addition to role flexibility there are a number of characteristics that people who are perceived to be good counsellors exhibit. In particular:

- □ empathy and detachment
- □ listening and interpreting
- □ leading and following
- □ getting behind the presenting issue
- □ suspending judgement
- □ moving at the speed of the learner.

Empathy and detachment

Apparent opposites, empathy and detachment are two sides of the same coin. The counsellor needs to be able to relate to the learner's issues and understand the learner's emotional perspective. The learner must feel that the counsellor is interested, respects and values him or her, that the counsellor cares. Yet at the same time the counsellor must avoid becoming entwined in the learner's issues or, even worse, taking part or total ownership of them. The counsellor can invite the learner to 'step outside his or her box' and look in with him or her only if the counsellor is already on the outside. This can be a difficult balance to maintain, and most people achieve proficiency in doing so only through practice. One of the signs of low proficiency in this aspect of counselling is a person's continually and mechanistically turning questions back on the learner because he or she is desperate not to take ownership of the issue. Always answering a question with a question or frequently saying 'And how do you feel about that?' rapidly becomes irritating and destroys both rapport and the learner's sense of confidence in the counsellor. A wide set of responses and the confidence to catch the ball in order to return it are important characteristics of the effective counsellor.

Listening and interpreting

Like the good coach, the effective counsellor develops strong listening skills. Analysis of what has been said – the linguistic cues, the emotional highlights, the revealing absences (what has *not* been said) – is a separate, parallel activity. It is a bit like learning to juggle and ride a bicycle at the same time: both activities demand a high degree of attention, and focusing too much on one can lead to dire failure in both. We covered some of the skills of listening in the chapter on coaching (Chapter 2) – these are all equally relevant to the counsellor. The skills of analysis are diverse and more difficult to define. They depend upon acquiring a broad set of models of behaviour and business processes against which to frame what the counsellor hears.

Leading and following

Helping someone else along the path to insight demands sensitivity in recognising when to point in the right direction ('Have you considered ...?' 'What if you ...?') and when to let the learner find his or her own path, giving encouragement along the way.

Getting behind the presenting issue

The counsellor needs a strong intuitive sense to recognise when there is more to an issue than appears on the surface. A problem raised by the learner may be just one small example of a common occurrence (for example, a recent altercation with a close friend may be one of many dramatic break-ups) or a small part of a larger issue. An example of the latter is a CEO's annoyance at a failure by the public relations manager. Further questioning by the counsellor revealed that the CEO had been unhappy with the PR manager's performance for some time but had done nothing about it. Why not? Because the CEO felt deeply uncomfortable about dealing with the press herself and was unwilling to face this bigger issue. Once the larger issue was in the open, both it and the presenting issue were quickly tackled. The PR manager was replaced; the new incumbent had the competence and confidence to coach the CEO in press relations; and the CEO soon found a natural talent for the task!

Figure 14 illustrates how this process of managing presented issues typically works. The counsellor questions the learner about the presenting issue and begins to form some insights into what the real (or more significant) issues might be. He or she uses that insight to question the learner more deeply about the presenting issue until the learner achieves the same or a similar insight. Once the real issue is open for debate, the learner and the counsellor can start to discuss practical options for dealing with it.

Figure 14
MANAGING PRESENTED ISSUES

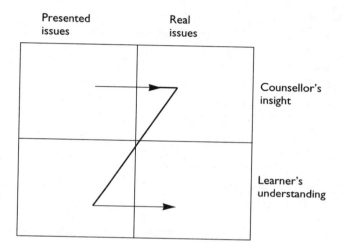

Presented
issues

Real
issues

Counsellor's
insight

Learner's
understanding

Suspending judgement

The difference between continuous analysis and judgement is that analysis should remain open-ended as long as the dialogue continues. Coming to a judgement implies that all the evidence is collated and assessed, and that a logical conclusion has emerged. The problem is, people's emotional lives are not logical. Indeed, almost any logic we attempt to overlay onto another person's behaviour or thinking will be at best a partial picture. Because we can never truly share another person's perspective in its entirety, effective counsellors never assume they 'know what the problem is'. Instead, they help the individual work through the issues until he or she comes to a personal conclusion. Only if that conclusion appears to contradict the available evidence does the counsellor continue to probe, trying to bring the learner to a greater depth of personal insight. Telling a learner 'Your issue is ...' undermines counselling by taking back ownership of the process.

Moving at the speed of the learner

It may seem obvious, but learners can progress through counselling only at a pace they can accommodate. This does not mean that they should necessarily feel comfortable – facing up to hard personal truths is inevitably painful, even if the initial pain does lead to subsequent relief – but there must be a balance between the learner's need to address issues and the natural desire to avoid the pain of doing so. That balance may change substantially as learners become more accustomed to opening the closed doors of their minds. Often the insight gained from counselling can add a sense of urgency to the learner development activity – being sure of knowing what you want to achieve and why can be a remarkable stimulus.

Psychometrics and counselling

In helping the learner gain self-understanding, any tool that sheds light on behaviour or aptitude can be useful. But psychometric tests, in particular, need to be treated with caution, even if they are well-validated. For a start, self-completed questionnaires tell learners only what they already believe about themselves. They reflect only the individual's *id*, not the full personality. (A more accurate picture is likely to emerge when the individual's perception is compared and contrasted with that of others who know him or her.) Another issue is that people's scores on some tests can change along with their lifestyles and workstyles over time – what you do eventually affects what you are!

For the counsellor, psychometrics can provide clues to behavioural issues for the learner. For example, overemphasis or rigidity in one or more learning or communication styles is potentially likely to cause problems in relationships with people who are inclined to emphasise opposite styles. Similarly, extreme scores for personality traits on the Myers-Briggs or 16PF indicators may suggest potential problems. However, few tests are sufficiently robust to be used as more than an indicator; they are rarely reliable enough to be used as a sole assessment. Moreover, unless the counsellor has been trained in interpretation of such data, there is a high risk of giving poor advice. Some workplace counsellors take an in-between course, advising the learner to seek professional interpretation through personality profiling (a mixture of psychometric testing and interview by a clinical psychologist) and then working through the psychologist's written report with the learner to relate it to workplace issues.

Conclusion

The need for workplace counselling is likely to grow rapidly in the de-layered organisation. Hierarchies and stable structures provided a certainty that was highly comforting. As that certainly erodes, people need greater support to test the ground on a multitude of business and personal decisions that would previously have been taken for them.

The counsellor role encompasses a range of behaviours including listening, empathising and being a sounding-board. But the broad aim is to help people gain the understanding to plan how they will achieve development or career objectives.

Ideally, every manager should have some competence at workplace counselling. In practice, many managers will not have sufficient self-understanding or interest in others to fulfil the role with sensitivity. Others may find it difficult to disengage, to separate their own needs and perceptions from those of the learner. The problem for the human resource profession, then, may be to find enough counsellors in the short and medium term, and to manage the promotion system in favour of people worth counselling competence.

5   THE NETWORKER/ FACILITATOR

Defining and describing a networker/facilitator

Of all the roles that people in organisations can adopt to help others with their learning, the networker/facilitator's is at the same time both the easiest to grasp intuitively and the most difficult to define. Experienced people in an organisation fall into the role naturally, even unconsciously, whenever they are asked 'Who would be the best person to contact about this or that issue?' Effective networker/facilitators recognise that they do not have all the answers, but they almost always 'know a man (or woman) who does'.

To fully understand this role it is important to recognise the difference between being simply a good networker and being a networker/facilitator. Good networkers are people who are adept at making connections – they have an instinctive understanding of who might at some stage be useful to know and an ability both to penetrate that person's network and to keep in touch. They understand that networks function on a currency of mutual interest or self-interest, so they spend time investing in establishing their own usefulness to other network members. (Sometimes this may simply be by virtue of who they can link those other members to.)

Good networker/facilitators go one step further. They actively recruit new people into the networks, even where doing so has no obvious, active benefit to them. They share their networks relatively openly with less experienced people, whose usefulness to the network may not yet be proven. The emphasis of their investment, then, is at least on establishing other people's value as much as their own. They perceive that exposure to different and wider networks is a major advantage in both self-managed learning and career self-management, and they recognise that they can help learners by helping them make their own connections.

In pursuing this path they bring benefits to all parties: the learner, the helper, the organisation and the network itself. The learner is able to multiply by many times the sources of advice and alternative experience available to him or her; the networker/facilitator enhances his or her reputation within the network as an active 'connector of souls'; the organisation is able to tap in, through the learner, to a much wider range of expertise within (and often also outside) the company to tackle specific issues; and the network gains yet more resources.

There are, however, also downsides for the networker/facilitator. Networking relationships that have been built up painstakingly for years may be wrecked if the referred learner abuses the opportunity. For example, a manager in a chemicals company passed on a young graduate who had an interest in joining another division to a very senior colleague in that division. The graduate's behaviour was highly presumptuous, however. Having observed the chatty and relaxed way in which the networker/facilitator spoke to the senior man, he presented himself in the same way and failed to react when the manager hinted several times that he had time restraints. The result was a distinct cooling in the original relationship, because the helper was perceived either to have failed to brief the younger person properly or to have failed in judgement about whether to make the link at all. So the helper's perceived value and reputation within the network – or at least that part of it – was damaged. As we shall see below, part of the skill of being an effective networker/facilitator is establishing when to trust the learner with one of your most valuable assets. Opening your networks to others is rather like handing over the keys of your new car: it pays to consider first how much confidence you have in the other person's driving ability and what the risks are if your judgement is ill-founded.

One other defining feature of networker/facilitators is also worth mentioning at this point. Although they are most commonly recognised for their access to *people*, they may also have access to a much wider web of *learning resources*. Directly or indirectly, they are likely to know about all sorts of opportunities inside and outside the organisation that may be of benefit to the learner:

- ☐ 'Did you know that finance is running a workshop for its own people on project budgeting? I'm sure the manager would be able to make a place for you, even though you're from another department, if you put up a good enough case.'
- ☐ 'If you're looking for exposure, have you considered writing an article for the trade periodical?'
- ☐ 'The local business school is always looking for experienced business people to discuss topics with the MBAs ...'
- ☐ 'I understand that the marketing director wants to set up a cross-company, cross-layer working party on integrating internal and external messages ...'

It is often the diversity and unexpectedness of these opportunities that makes them so useful. Networker/facilitators do not provide these titbits with any suggestion of obligation on learners to take advantage of them – they expect learners to make their own choices, according to their own criteria. Unlike the sponsoring role, where the opportunity is at least partly, if not entirely, in the helper's gift and where the sponsor will actively intervene, in this role the seizing of opportunities rests squarely with the learners. The networker/facilitators' most active contribution is to make introductions where the learners need help in doing so. Compared to coach or guardian this is a very passive role.

The nature of networks
Networking: Learning from and influencing through multiple relationships

Everyone at work operates to a greater or lesser extent through networks: people outside your team on whom you rely to contribute some aspect of the total task. Academics attempt to define networks in a variety of ways, but the simplest perspective is by function. All networks exist either to acquire and distribute information or to acquire and exercise influence. A single network may have either or both of these purposes.

Information networks enable people to understand what is

going on in the organisation. At their crudest they form the grapevine – rapid, often unreliable and random. At their most sophisticated they are a part of the strategic thinking of the organisation – sharing thinking and concepts so they can be tested out and redrafted before becoming public knowledge. Alternatively they may be more overt: semi-formal groupings, such as e-mail special-interest groups.

Most organisations involve many separate but interconnected information networks. They invariably include a number of people who are able to provide short-cuts to information that would otherwise take ages to appear, or who have the perspective to identify the patterns behind what looks to be unconnected data. For example, the foreman in charge of the goods outwards bay is in a unique position to assess how well the company is doing at the moment. Similarly, the managing director's secretary has privileged access to a great deal of information. Although she has to act, of course, within limits of discretion and confidentiality, she may be able to steer someone wanting guidance on what tack to take when presenting an issue to the board.

Influence networks help you get things done. One of the simplest illustrations is persuading the accounts department to push through a payment to a favoured supplier. To go through the departmental head or through formal channels may take considerable time and effort. If you are on good terms with the clerk who processes the accounts and can ask him or her directly to bring that file to the top of the pile, things are likely to happen much more quickly. The clerk is, in effect, part of your influence network. The currency with which you repay them will vary but could, for example, be in making sure that your department gets its monthly figures in on time.

Academic studies that talk of 'trust networks'[1] to some extent miss the point. Trust is one of the processes that enable the network to function. The fact that we trust some people more than others, and that other people's trust in us also varies, simply determines the dynamics of that network. Moreover, trust works on several levels:

☐ trust in your goodwill and intentions
☐ trust in your integrity (eg ability to maintain confidences)

□ trust in your judgement *relevant to the issue or task in question.*

No single metaphor is able to describe the richness of a well-functioning network. Comparisons with the world-wide web remind us that few if any networks are isolated. They leak at the edges, where people are members of yet other networks, whose members in turn. ... A spider's web has a clear centre, just as individuals build their own networks around their personal priorities. Yet the spider typically waits at the side of the web, listening to the vibrations, sensing opportunities as they arise, and moving swiftly to take advantage of them. In the same way, although you may consciously construct a network around your specific needs, it will function only if other people participate. Being in the centre of a network may not be the best place to pick up the vibrations.

The club metaphor is also helpful. Most clubs have an active core of people who come and go over the years and make things happen. They also have members who are happy to volunteer or be volunteered from time to time but want no part of the responsibilities. And they have a third group who pay their dues but rarely, if ever, participate. The same groupings can be seen in almost any network.

Clubs also tend to have rules about membership. You have to be invited in by recommendation of existing members. Your entry must, if it does not enhance the reputation of the club, at least not undermine it. The same is broadly true of networks: to be accepted by the other members you must be able to demonstrate the relevance of your presence in the net and the value you will bring to it. How these factors are assessed depends upon the 'currency' that drives the network. If you are not a source of information or influence, why are you there? New members may be accepted in anticipation of their being able to contribute in the future, but the more mature the network, the more difficult it is for a neophyte to join. The networker/facilitator has a key role to play here in acting as the 'club secretary' – helping the learner make his or her own case for being allowed into the network.

Learning networks

Learning networks are a subset of information networks. They consist of the principal people from whom you can usefully learn. Within my learning net, for example, are a number of people who are (technically) direct reports, an academic supervisor, a host of working colleagues, some key staff at a charity, people whom I mentor, and several 'elder statesmen' of business.

In recent years, I have asked dozens of managers to map their learning nets (see below for more on network mapping) and to score each relationship by the potential for learning and the efficiency (opportunity v actual use) with which they tap into each of those sources of learning. The result, by and large, is as depressing as might be expected. Most of the potential for learning remains as just potential.

Putting one's learning net on paper or screen forces people to think about how they manage learning from others. In some cases it has caused managers to radically change the way they approach their teams. For the manager to ask at team meetings 'What can you teach me this week?' may mean a significant change of style, but it opens up great possibilities for learning on both sides.

In general, the wider the learning net, the more extensive the learning an individual is able to access. For a typical manager that net might include peers, direct reports, their line bosses and other people at the same level, off-line mentors, and people in the relevant professional associations. But it could also include university staff, people in departments within the business that they would normally have no contact with, journalists (who by nature and profession are very free with information, especially to those people who keep them informed in turn) or simply close friends who work in totally different organisations or occupations. The more narrowly we define our learning net, the more narrow the scope of our learning.

Four styles of networker/facilitator

You will not be surprised to find that the networker/facilitator role – like the other helping roles – has a number of styles,

Figure 15
NETWORKER/FACILITATOR STYLES

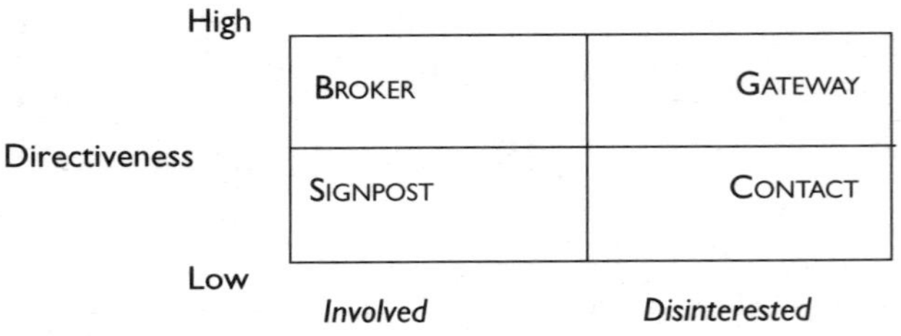

High

	BROKER	GATEWAY
Directiveness	SIGNPOST	CONTACT

Low

Involved   *Disinterested*

which we can call GATEWAY, SIGNPOST, CONTACT and BROKER. As in the other roles, the degree of directiveness forms one defining dimension, although we are now well towards the non-directive end of the scale. We can define directiveness in this sense more in terms of how active or passive the helper is in linking the learner to other sources of learning.

The second defining axis of style concerns the helper's personal involvement and interest in the outcomes from his or her interaction with the learner – ie to what extent is this a gift or an exchange?

Gateway

The gateway responds to learners' requests by putting them in touch with other people. He or she uses his or her own name and influence to make connections on a learner's behalf. In doing so, he or she places some obligations on the learner to use those introductions sensitively. The gateway's behaviour is very different from that of a sponsor because he or she takes responsibility only for vetting the learner before the learner achieves access to the network. Once the connection is made, the learner is on his or her own.

Signpost

The signpost has extensive knowledge and networks, and gives the learner a range of options to pursue. He or she helps the learner develop criteria for selecting between the many options. For example:

- ☐ Who is the best person to approach about this issue?
- ☐ Which of these learning opportunities will do my career most good?

But the signpost does not attempt to influence the learner's choice. In effect, he or she says 'I have a great deal of general knowledge – both the big-picture perspective and small-picture detail. I'll share it with you and point out the various directions you can go, but you own the decision.' Nor does the signpost normally make the connection for the learner: it is the learner's business what he or she does with the information that has been given.

Contact

The contact is a 'distant friend' who provides information or connections when asked. Many contacts would not even recognise that a helping relationship existed beyond the normal day-to-day routine of responding to requests. As a helping style, the contact is simply available as needed. The helper would never dream of approaching the learner or suggesting a meeting – he or she simply responds as needed.

In practice, the contact is often the person to whom the gateway or sponsor typically passes the learner for specific information or advice. What takes place is a network transaction rather than the development of a strong personal relationship. This is not to denigrate the value of this style. Managers in organisations do not have the time to develop deep and meaningful relationships with everyone who might need their help. And the learner does not need to get close to everyone in his or her learning net. The mature self-learner has multiple sources within his or her learning net for most of whom the relationship will rarely be more than an occasional transaction.

Broker

The broker is an active networker who sees the networks as a critical part of his or her own resource management. Typically a wheeler-dealer, the broker thrives on putting people together. The agenda, however, may be driven largely by the broker's own needs and interests. He or she may be less concerned with helping others to learn than with making the network work and fulfilling his or her own or the organisation's objectives through other people. The fact that this interest fits well with the development needs of people whom he or she invites into the network is almost coincidental. Nonetheless, the broker does provide a highly focused, pragmatic resource for the learner to expand his or her networks.

Choosing between networker/facilitator styles

The choice of which style to use depends, as always, on the situation and the needs of the learner. The more self-assured and network-competent the learner, the more hands-off approach her or she will require. But the style choice also depends on whether the relationship lies solely within the networking/facilitation box or is a much broader relationship, encompassing other boxes in the 'helping to learn' model. The closer and more complex the relationship, the less appropriate the contact style will be, for example. A broker style might fit more appropriately with a relationship that emphasised the guardian role.

Fortunately, the basic skills seem to be much the same, whichever style you decide is appropriate.

The skills of an effective networker/facilitator

When questioning mentors and line-manager coaches about how they fulfil their helping role as networker/facilitators, the responses almost always fall into four core skills:

- □ managing their own networks
- □ managing their own learning
- □ opening their networks to others
- □ helping others to develop their own networks.

These skills are intricately linked. A consciousness of their own networks and what they personally need from them encourages them to assist others in the knowledge that at least some of those people will, in the short or long term, become valuable information or influence nodes in return. Because information and influence needs constantly evolve, the only way to maintain the quality and topicality of a network is to keep expanding it by inviting other people in. As your needs change, you may also move the centre of your web, so old core contacts move farther out towards the edges.

People who are recognised as good networkers and facilitators tend to be strong communicators, with high sociability and an instinct for identifying swiftly the drivers and values of people they meet. At an extreme they can appear quite ruthless, evaluating everyone they encounter in terms of their usefulness. (This presumably eventually has an impact on the degree of trust they are able to command in others, and hence in the quality of network transactions, although this may be compensated for in quantity. I say 'presumably' because there is little, if any, objective study of this aspect of networking.)

Managing your own networks

Good networkers both maintain their existing contacts and spend a lot of time developing new ones. They view each person they meet as a possible introduction to others whom they would like to meet even more. They also have a relatively clear perception of what they can offer to potential network partners – usually a combination of expert knowledge, extensive contacts within specific spheres to which others will value access and/or an ability to contribute original thinking. They rarely, if ever, charge for putting people in their network in touch with each other. (The main exceptions are head-hunters and other kinds of broker, for whom the network is a commercial vehicle. Not surprisingly, this tends to make for a different kind of relationship. Part of the exchange between the head-hunter and people in his or her network is information for influence. When the head-hunter rings asking for suggestions, managers will typically try to be helpful, drawing on their own networks, in the hope that the head-hunter will one day repay them with an introduction that *they* will want to follow up.)

Some of the practical measures accomplished networkers take include:

□ keeping a clear and constantly updated record of all useful contacts

□ maintaining regular contact with each of these on appropriate cycles

□ using a relatively wide range of ways of communicating to network contacts.

Taking each of these measures in turn, good networkers typically record much more than name and contact details. They also record with whom the contact can link them. At its most sophisticated, such databases can contain several thousand names, along with some form of linkage between them. People who work for the same company, belong to the council of the same industry federation, or who share the same needs for specific kinds of information – all this information is valuable in making practical use of the network.

At an even more sophisticated level it makes sense to classify people in your networks according to their importance, or according to how you might expect to use them. One useful method of classification around the latter is as:

□ direct contacts – people you maintain a relationship with entirely for its own sake: ie who are of minimal value in introducing you to others

□ direct links – people who can connect you with a small number of others for specific purposes

□ multiple links – people who can connect you with a large number of others whose usefulness will become clear only as you (or the learner) develop specific needs or interests.

Maintaining the network is equally important. Regular catching up, timed loosely according to importance, helps you establish how your network contacts' usefulness has changed – for example, does a change of job make them less or more viable as a source of information or influence? At its simplest and crudest this aspect of networking can be seen in the car salesperson who finds out from customers how frequently they change their car and ensures that he or she makes contact a few months beforehand to rebuild the relationship. (It is still remarkably rare, even though it is often quoted as standard practice!)

More importantly, though, regular contact ensures that the relationship develops on the personal rather than simply on the transactional level. The effective networker makes a point of initiating such contacts and always makes a gift of knowledge or some other currency the receiver may value. This may be a lead to an interesting business possibility, a clipping from a newspaper, a summary from a report the other person may not have seen, or, if all else fails, a simple intro-duction to one or two people the other person might find it useful to meet. In constantly giving, the networker creates the goodwill or relationship capital to receive the other person's attention and help, when it is needed.

While most accomplished networkers favour one or two methods of keeping in touch – some, for example, focus their efforts on breakfast meetings every day – they typically also use a variety of approaches, recognising that different people respond to different media. The preferred style of contact is another factor that can be built into the networking database.

Managing your own learning

The facilitator part of the networker/facilitator role is about helping the learner take charge of his or her own learning. Self-managed learning is such a vast subject on its own that I do not intend to explore it in great detail here. Some basic principles are worth establishing, however. In particular, it seems that:

□ people who are effective at managing their own learning tend to be better at helping others manage theirs

□ the more sensitive you are for learning opportunities for yourself, the more likely you are to recognise learning opportunities for others in your network

□ the more practice you get at thinking through choices between learning opportunities, the better you are likely to be in helping other people make such choices.

Managing your own learning effectively requires, among other things:

□ creation of sufficient reflective space to think through both what you have learned and what you need to learn

□ clear learning goals, both for immediate work tasks and longer-term career development; and beyond the working environment into wider life goals of intellectual growth, leisure, physical well-being and, perhaps, spiritual development

☐ enlisting the help of others, both in giving advice or knowledge and in providing feedback that will stimulate reflection

☐ maintaining a record (learning log) to assess progress against learning goals

☐ seeking opportunities for serendipitous learning – situations that will open your eyes to new learning potential.

By developing these behaviours in themselves, networker/ facilitators often become remarkably effective role models. By emulating their approaches, learners may become rapidly empowered and better able to access the variety of helping resources around them.

Opening your networks to others

The point has already been made that opening networks to others requires mutual trust, especially if the relationship between the existing network partners is sensitive and has required long and careful cultivation. In the end, however, you have to open up your network to others if you want them to join and bring their contacts too. The investment may take years – a young graduate will have a very limited network and relative paucity of information or influence to trade – and not all constituent elements may pay off, but that is the nature of investment.

In opening networks to other people, the accomplished networker/facilitator:

☐ assesses the degree of trust and risk involved

☐ spends time exploring the relevance and need of the learner – is this the best way to accomplish the learning goal?

☐ helps the learner think through how to approach the contact (Directly or indirectly? By telephone, or letter, or in person – say, after a meeting? What will convince the contact to make the investment of time?)

☐ subsequently reviews the event with the learner (Did he or she get what was wanted? Was the contact positive and welcoming, and if not, why not? What did the contact get out of the meeting? How would he or she tackle it differently next time? What further contacts did he or she make as a result?)

Added together, all of this takes a lot more time than saying, 'Well, why don't you talk to Jane in legal about that?' The pay-off lies in the depth of learning by the person being helped, the opportunity to strengthen the relationship with the learner, and the gradual extension of the networker's own contacts and understanding of the organisation.

Helping a learner develop his or her own network and networking skills

The sooner the networker/facilitator can transfer the skills of networking and self-managed learning, the sooner he or she can move on to the next relationship that will develop his or her own networks. So it is in everyone's interest to make it happen as swiftly and easily as possible. A practical short step is to help the learner begin *network-mapping.*

Network-mapping is a straightforward tool for assessing the state of a person's current networks and planning how to develop them. The starting-point is the here and now, the learner's existing networks. These can be mapped out by listing the critical tasks in his or her current work that need either information or influence from other people to be done really well. For each task the learner needs to consider, 'Who do I get this information from?' and/or 'How do I persuade people to make that happen?'

In the example shown in Figure 16, network-mapping reveals two large holes in the manager's networks, both of which may affect his or her performance. The lack of a mediator between the manager and the project review committee makes it more difficult to put his or her case. Failure to keep up with the latest technical developments may result in lost opportunities for cost savings and/or client satisfaction.

Among the ground rules of drawing up a network map are the following:

Figure 16
EXAMPLE OF A NETWORK MAP

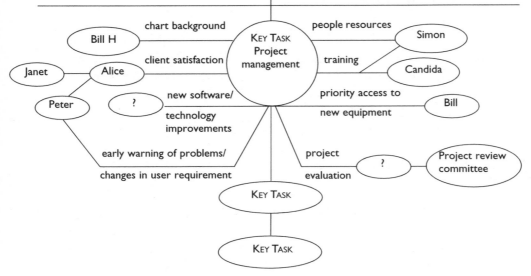

Information: Who do I get information from? | **Influence**: Whose help do I need to get things done?

□ A resource may be a person, a database, an institution (eg a professional body) or another network.

□ The same resource may appear several times in the network map under different guises.

□ It often pays to have more than one resource for important needs (perhaps many).

□ The map may be kept relatively simple by keeping the basic tasks simple – if it gets too complex, break the task up into smaller chunks.

Just this simple activity is often enough to make people realise that they are not getting the quality of support they require from co-workers, and to question why. If the information they receive is poor, is it because the source is inadequately informed or incompetent? Or is it because the relationship is inadequate? In the former case, the answer may be to seek better or more direct sources of information. In the latter, it may be to change the nature of the relationship by increasing its value to the network source – ie what currency do they want to be repaid in? Or it may be necessary to invest in building greater trust with those people.

The next step is to consider how to expand and develop the existing networks. Who *should* be in them? Why aren't they? What can I do to bring them in? Whose help can I enlist?

With this practice behind them, people are usually ready to turn their attention to their broader learning and career-management needs: what do they want to achieve? Based on this understanding, what sort of network do they need to develop? Whom do they really want to reach? Defining the network in these terms typically establishes major gaps where there are few or no links between the learner and the people he or she wants to connect to.

In making these classifications, it is as well not to dismiss people simply as direct contacts – and therefore of limited resource value – too easily. In a recent experiment in networking, my consulting colleague Jenny Sweeney and I created a networking market for a group of graduate recruits who had been with their company between 12 and 24 months. Although they had met together on a number of occasions for induction and training events, the graduates had never really considered how much a resource they could be for each other. Within the market, the graduates could either request information about an area of the company about which they would like to know or in which they would like to work, or they could offer information about areas of the company of which they had experience or knowledge. It rapidly became clear that, between them, they had a substantial store of knowledge about the company and could provide valuable contacts and advice for each other.

In practice, few of us are routinely as disciplined in managing our networks as this model would imply. Carried to the extreme, these networking behaviours could absorb most of a manager's productive time. However, being just a bit more disciplined can benefit out of all proportion to the effort expended both the manager and the person whom he or she is trying to help.

Conclusion

The networker/facilitator role is the most difficult to define or to allocate formally. By and large it 'just happens'. But, by bringing it within the formal skills set of people who help others to learn, we can enrich all the other helping roles while increasing the helpers' ability to manage their own learning and performance.

End-note

1 KRACKHARDT D. *and* HANSON J. 'Informal networks: the company behind the chart *Harvard Business Review*, 1993.

6 MENTORING: THE INTEGRATING ROLE

Definitions and models of mentoring

Mentoring is one of the most powerful developmental approaches available to individuals and organisations. Certainly, the spread of planned mentoring programmes first in the USA, then in Europe and Asia-Pacific, has been rapid. But it has not always been successful. Moreover, any attempt to establish practical guidelines about achieving success by reading the extensive literature on mentoring tends to founder in confusion over what is being described. Mentoring is sometimes used as another term for coaching, for counselling, for tutoring, for small business consulting – even as a synonym for the semi-disciplinary role of probation officer.

Much of the widespread confusion about what is and is not mentoring comes from the fact that there are two distinct schools of thought. The traditional, North American concept of mentoring is embodied by someone older and more powerful, who expects loyalty in return for advice, guidance and a helping hand. In this personification the mentor may be the person's line manager. The term *protégé* is typically used to describe the relationship, which places relatively little emphasis on learning (by either party) and a lot on assistance with making the right career moves.

By contrast, the European concept of mentoring assumes that the mentor has more *experience* rather than more *power*. Indeed, a characteristic of an effective mentoring relationship is the 'parking' of any power differences so that the two can deal as equals. As a result, European mentors are almost always off-line, not least because it is difficult to be very open to someone who has the power to influence your pay, status and general well-being. The purpose of the relationship is primarily learning or development, although a result of learning may well be better career management by the *mentee*.

Figure 17
THE EUROPEAN MODEL OF MENTORING

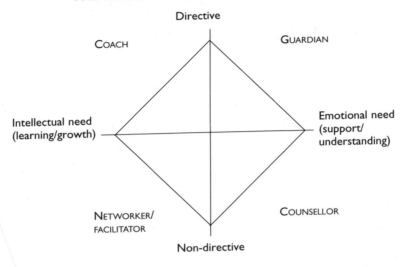

('Mentee' is an awful word but the best we have, other than 'learner'. The European Mentoring Centre has a standing award of a magnum of champagne – unclaimed for six years – for anyone proposing a widely acceptable alternative word!) The European Mentoring Centre's catch-all definition of mentoring is 'Off-line help by one person to another in making significant transitions in knowledge, work or thinking'.

In practice, neither model is 'pure' when it comes to application in the real world. The needs of the mentee may well be such that the relationship includes some measure of sponsorship, for example. And different cultures – both national and corporate – will require a different emphasis on what kind of support is offered and taken. To put mentoring into context, we have to see it as drawing upon all of the other styles of helping to learn. The European model produces a picture something like the one shown in Figure 17.

The traditional US model, by contrast, focuses mainly in the top two boxes of the diagram (see Figure 18).

Because this book is about helping others to learn, rather than about helping others with their careers, it is the European

Figure 18
THE TRADITIONAL US MODEL OF MENTORING

Directive

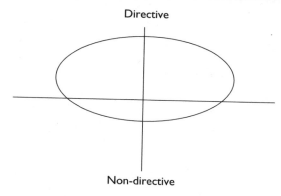

Non-directive

model that the rest of this chapter focuses on. The role of the developmental mentor is complex because he or she has to have at least a reasonable level of ability in all four of the other roles: coach, counsellor, guardian and networker/facilitator. The sensitivity to know when to move into each role is perhaps the most important characteristic of an effective mentor. In Chapter 1 we explored the differences in style between various kinds of learning transfer. The learning that takes

Table 5
DEVELOPMENTAL MENTORING

Developmental mentoring involves:		
Always ...	*Sometimes ...*	*Never ...*
listening with empathy	using coaching behaviours	discipline
sharing experience	using counselling behaviours	appraisal
mutual learning	challenging assumptions	assessment for a third party
professional friendship	being a role model	supervision
developing insight through reflection	opening doors	
being a sounding-board		
encouraging		

Figure 19
A VALUE CHAIN

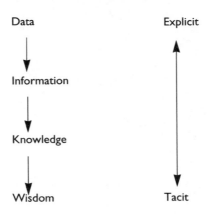

place in mentoring is qualitatively different from that to be expected from teaching, tutoring or coaching. In broad terms, teaching and tutoring are about acquiring knowledge; coaching about skills; mentoring about acquiring wisdom. What transfers between mentor and mentee can rarely be found in books. It is personalised and adapted to the circumstances, drawing on a mixture of accumulated experience and contextual understanding.

One way of describing wisdom is by what it enables you do to. Data becomes useful when it is organised into information. Information becomes useful when it can be reconstructed into knowledge, which implies some degree of understanding of how information can be applied. When knowledge can be extrapolated beyond one set of circumstances, with understanding of broad principles, and linked to other relevant knowledge, it becomes wisdom (see Figure 19).

In the organisational context, wisdom may be to do with the politics of the job, how to operate within the system and the rules without being unduly restrained by them, how to interpret likely sequences of events, and so on. It can be acquired only by extensive personal experience and observation, by tapping into the wisdom of others, or by a mixture of the two.

Because developmental mentoring is essentially a sharing

of wisdom, one of its distinguishing characteristics as a 'helping to learn' process is that it is a two-way street. Whenever we evaluate mentoring schemes that have been well-designed and implemented, we find that the mentors have gained as much and sometimes more than the mentees. This mutuality of benefit stems from the requirement in mentoring to delve deeply into professional and personal issues: in helping someone else to greater understanding, the mentor also undergoes a voyage of discovery.

The mechanism by which this happens is charted in Figure 20. Essentially, the learner presents an issue and seeks the mentor's guidance. The effective mentor will typically hold back from giving advice or recounting from experience until the learner has been helped to think the issues through from his or her own perspective. But eventually the point will come when it becomes appropriate to tap into the mentor's wisdom.

Let's say the issue is *How do I get my reports accepted by the executive committee?*, addressed to a mentor who him- or herself has few problems in this regard. The mentor thinks back to any times when he or she had similar quandaries and how they were resolved; he or she also tries to put into words precisely what he or she does in preparing and presenting a report that makes the difference. For example, the mentor may spend time with key players on the committee, to manage their expectations. What happens here is the articulation of a process that has probably never before been mapped. It is a classic translation of *tacit* or implicit knowledge (or wisdom) to *explicit* knowledge.

This process of articulation obliges the mentor to think about what he or she does from a critical perspective that would rarely occur otherwise. If the mentor's process model is sound, explaining it to someone else re-inforces it in his or her mind. As a result, consistency in applying the good-practice rules that he or she is enunciating may well increase. If the process model is not sound, here is an opportunity for critical thinking around an area in which there can be improvement. If the learner does not understand the process or challenges its validity, a dialogue opens out that may have potential value to both parties. Even if the learner accepts the

Figure 20
HOW MENTORS LEARN FROM MENTEES

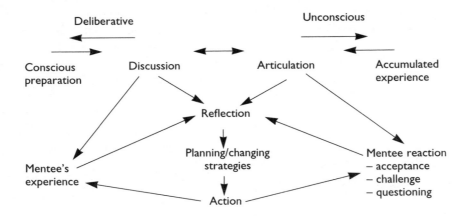

process uncritically, there is an opportunity for the mentor to learn when the guidance is put into practice. If the learner's attempt to follow the process is unsuccessful, or only partly successful, the pair will discuss the reasons why. Frequently, this will lead to questioning the process itself, or at least its generalisation. The question W*hy does this seem to work for me but not for other people?* can stimulate the mentor to valuable self-learning.

We shall examine the issue of benefits to mentors (and other parties) later in this chapter. Before doing so, however, it is logical to discuss what mentors do, and how this differentiates them from people in other helping roles.

What do mentors do?

The glib answer, 'Respond to the mentee's needs', is nonetheless pretty accurate. The core skill of being a mentor is knowing when and how to shift behavioural style within the boundaries of the relationship. The diamond shape at the centre of Figure 17 on page 88 (see also Figure 3, page 10) defines the broad context in which mentors operate. The mentor may operate as role model, sounding-board, critical friend, or any of the other behaviours shown.

At the same time, the mentor needs to recognise the boundary of the relationship – the point at which mentoring ceases and a different type of relationship begins. So, for example, while he or she may use some coaching style behaviours, the mentor will not set development goals for the mentee, nor will he or she usually give direct feedback about how he or she has observed the mentee at work. (The one exception to the latter statement would be when the mentee asks to 'dry run' a presentation or discussion with the mentor.) Similarly, the developmental mentor will not adopt a sponsorship role, and will not normally provide therapeutic counselling, even if he or she has the skills to do so. To move into therapeutic counselling would radically change the nature of the relationship: when faced with such a situation, effective mentors recognise the boundaries and help the learner to get specialist help.

As yet uncompleted research explores the importance of clarity of expectations by both mentor and mentee in managing the relationship. The initial investigations suggest that the expectations both parties bring to the relationship will have a significant impact on their behaviours towards each other. Given that 'behaviour breeds behaviour', any serious mismatches of expec-

Figure 21
AN EXPECTATIONS/OUTCOMES MODEL

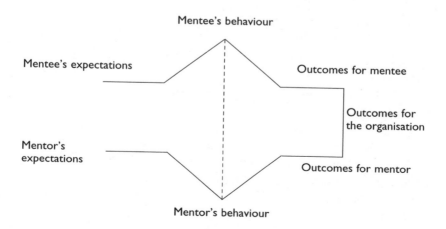

tation are likely to cause noise in the system, with the result that neither side achieves the desired outcomes (Figure 21).

A powerful example of this principle comes from a mentoring scheme I helped to introduce in Brunei. The mentors were mainly expatriates and the mentees mainly local citizens. Both were asked to map on the directive/non-directive intellectual/emotional matrix the shape of the relationship they expected. The mentors depicted a relationship heavy on self-managed learning by the mentee, with very little hands-on help; the mentees were near-unanimous in expecting exactly the opposite. The contrast, when presented to the mentors, prompted one of them to exclaim 'Now I see why I have so many problems getting my direct reports to learn.' Each mentoring pair subsequently negotiated a compromise set of mutual expectations somewhere between the supporting, sponsoring behaviours instinctive within the mentees' culture and the more challenge-driven, hands-off approach with which the mentors felt most comfortable.

The range of developmental mentoring behaviours has been covered bit by bit in the previous chapters, but it may be useful to bring the most important together here:

- □ collaborating, involving doing things with the mentee – eg preparing a presentation together
- □ goal-setting, involving helping the mentee set viable yet stretching personal goals
- □ challenging, involving pushing mentees to think more deeply about issues, particularly how they perceive themselves and their relationships with others
- □ acting as a critical friend to tell the mentee what other people are too polite or embarrassed to say
- □ listening and questioning
- □ acting as a sounding-board: someone the mentee can use to talk through ideas and plans without fear of ridicule; who will give constructive and impartial feedback
- □ guiding: explaining how the organisation works, what the politics are; helping the mentee develop 'worldly wise' attitudes

- acting as a role model: providing an example for the younger person to follow
- acting as a bridge: someone who actively seeks out useful contacts for the mentee and advises on how to approach them
- acting as a network catalyst: someone who stimulates the mentee into making his or her own network connections.

When and how the mentor uses each behaviour will also be influenced by the evolution of the relationship. All successful mentoring relationships go through several phases, as shown in Figure 22, and each phase tends to require a slightly different emphasis of behaviours.

Figure 22
EVOLUTION OF THE MENTORING RELATIONSHIP

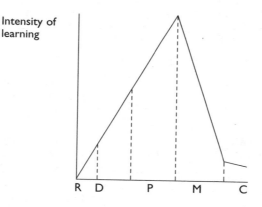

R   Rapport-building is about developing trust and comfort with each other.
D   Direction-setting is about setting goals for the relationship.
    Goals may (usually will) evolve with the relationship.
P   Progress-making is the most intensive stage, where experimentation and learning proceed rapidly.
M   Maturation is when the relationship becomes more mutual in terms of learning and support. The mentee gradually becomes more and more self-reliant.

C Close-down is when the formal relationship ends. In most successful mentoring relationships there is an informal continuity on a equal basis.

Mentoring and learning styles

According to Kolb, Rubin and McIntyre (writing in *Organisational Psychology*, Hemel Hempstead, Prentice Hall, 1974), learning from experience takes place in four stages.

Stage 1 is the experience itself. Mentors can help by directing mentees towards relevant experiences.

Stage 2 is one of examination and reflection. The mentor can help the mentee to recognise experiences worth reflecting on and to analyse what exactly happened and why.

Stage 3 involves making wider sense of the experience. Here the mentor helps by pooling his or her experience and knowledge of the context with that of the mentee. He or she helps the mentee to see the bigger picture and understand the motivations of other people. The danger here is that the mentor will attempt to do all the thinking rather than be drawn out by the mentee.

Stage 4 is to plan how to make use of the learning and understanding acquired. Here the mentee uses the mentor as a sounding-board, and the mentor stimulates the mentee to consider a wider range of planning options.

Who makes an effective mentor?

The breadth of the mentoring role means that effective mentors are more difficult to come by than almost any other learning resource. Although some companies have adopted 'all-comer' mentoring schemes, the limitation upon them will always be finding sufficient mentors of sufficient calibre. At the very basic level, potential mentors should be people who have:

☐ an interest in developing others

☐ an interest in continuing to develop themselves

☐ reasonably good explaining skills, particularly in terms of expressing complex ideas and/or making their tacit knowledge explicit

☐ good listening ability (effective mentors typically talk for about 20 per cent of the time, encouraging the mentee to do most of the talking)

☐ a broader perspective than the mentees'

☐ generally good behavioural skills

☐ integrity

☐ a sense of humour (absolutely essential in the eyes of mentees!).

It could be argued that everything on this list is an important requirement for an effective manager. However, the mentor will tend to have *strengths* in most of these areas, rather than simply be functionally competent in them.

At a more advanced level – say, the professional mentor – the skills base would also include a very good understanding of both behaviour management and business management; the ability to use conceptual models to help the learner build his or her own understanding; and a very high level of self-awareness (which probably explains the great scarcity of competent professionals in this area).

Who makes an effective mentee?

Although in a previous book I argued that *Everyone Needs a Mentor* (2nd edn, London, Institute of Personnel and Development, 1991), the reality is that not everyone can make effective use of the opportunities a developmental mentor can offer. This may be because of their situation (which may change) or because of their temperament. It appears that people with a high *internal* locus of control (ie people who perceive that they can and do influence their environment, and that their future is very much in their own hands) are more likely to get substantial benefit out of developmental mentoring than those who believe their fate rests in others' hands (ie with a high *external* locus of control). The stronger people's attraction is towards self-managed learning and taking control of their own lives, the more they are likely to attract and keep a mentor – the more rapid progress will be, and the more committed the mentor.

In theory, people with a high external locus of control should benefit greatly from having a sponsoring style of mentor or a directive coach. After all, they *expect* to have things done for them but they may find it difficult to acquire such a mentor because sponsors, too, tend to seek out ambitious, self-confident, inner-locus people as protégés. Moreover, it is in the learner's own – and the organisation's – best interests to move his or her attitude set far more towards self-reliance.

One option for these people – who may make up the bulk of certain groups, such as low achievers – is to provide counselling as a first step towards taking greater charge of their own learning. In the less difficult cases it may even be appropriate for the organisation to arrange mentoring relationships where the primary purpose, at least to begin with, is to effect a change of attitude towards self-reliance. Practical experience suggests that this will work only when the mentor is particularly competent and when the learner recognises the need to change. Building the learner's confidence that he or she *can* change then becomes one of the mentor's initial and most challenging tasks.

When I ask groups of existing or potential mentors to describe what they are looking for in a mentee, the resulting picture invariably is one of someone so perfect they scarcely need a mentor. The reality is that both mentor and mentee come as they are, as imperfect human beings with many faults and foibles. The recognition by the mentor that most faults are simply misdirected or overused strengths helps to put the issues into perspective. For example, if mentees are too aggressive, the mentor can help them channel the energy in more constructive ways, raising their ability to recognise when aggressiveness is dysfunctional and unhelpful to themselves and others. The most difficult behaviour mentors report having to cope with (outside personality disorder) is what has variously been described as 'the pudding' or 'the hostile witness': the person who responds only briefly, who never opens up, who never allows his or her emotions to break through. The issue here is often one of establishing sufficient trust, which can happen only with great patience on the part of the mentor.

Within the normal run of a mentoring relationship, however, the clearer both parties are about the purpose of the getting together and about the kind of behaviours each expects of the other, the more smoothly it will run. This does not mean that it will be all sweetness and light. The process of digging into issues can release a great deal of indignation ('How dare she ask me that!'), self-recrimination and frustration, all of which must be dealt with as they occur. As long as this is perceived by both sides to be within the expected boundaries of the relationship, then it will help towards delivering the learning goals.

The expected behaviours for the learner can be mapped in exactly the same way as for the mentor, as Table 6 illustrates. Whichever role-box the relationship is in, the mentee will gain greatest benefit if he or she shows the appropriate behaviours. Not all the behaviours listed in the table are appropriate to developmental mentoring, however. For example, being ingratiating or overdependent is often a natural outcome of a

Table 6
A TYPOGRAPHY OF MENTEE BEHAVIOURS

COACHEE	ACOLYTE
Seeking for goals to be set	Demonstrates compliance/ ingratiation (lets mentor set agenda)
Positive attitude to difficult feedback	Seeks approval
Openness to new ideas	Demonstrates loyalty
Commitment to set and achieve own goals	Uses mentor as role model
	Seeks advice
Seeks help in developing contacts	Demonstrates trust in opening up issues for discussion
Brings own first thinking to meetings	Willing to explore own feelings
Sets own agenda	Seeks frequent reassurance
Has multiple mentors	Becomes dependent
SELF-MANAGED LEARNER	**TRUTH-SEEKER**

relationship between a strong sponsor and a weak protégé. Knowing which behaviours are desirable and which are not is a firm starting-point for behaving appropriately within the relationship. Where possible, this should form an important part of mentee training.

Managing the mentoring programme

One of the paradoxes of planned mentoring is that it involves informal relationships within a formal framework. Some studies have suggested that all mentoring should be informal and that *ad hoc* relationships work better than planned ones. However, these studies fail to carry conviction on several counts. One is that they fail to understand the dynamics of *ad hoc* mentoring – in particular, that you may have to kiss a lot of frogs before you find your ideal mentor in this way, which makes comparisons statistically questionable. Another is that it is easy to confuse rapport (relatively easy to achieve between two people of similar interests and background) with results. Very few of these studies focus on real outcomes for the mentee, and of those that do, most ignore the issue of outcomes for the mentor.

The arguments in favour of a planned programme or scheme are powerful. Left to their own devices, mentors will tend to seek mentees who remind them of themselves some years before. There can be a strong temptation to try to relive their careers through a younger person. The assertion 'My job is to prevent them from making the same mistakes I did' pushes the relationship heavily towards the directive. The mentor who sees the role in this way is, in effect, taking from the learner the opportunity to learn from his or her own mistakes. One of the common grounds for quitting expressed by graduates who have left companies is the unwelcome attention of a more senior person who takes too active a role in managing their career.

Mentees left to themselves tend to seek mentors who are more powerful and can influence their careers rather than people from whom they can learn. The two aspects may be irreconcilable in the same person – powerful high-flyers often have relatively little interest in developing others because their energies are focused on their own advancement.

Informal mentoring tends to marginalise minorities and other groups who do not fit the mainstream mould. Hence the rapid increase of corporate mentoring schemes aimed at women, non-whites and the disabled. Such schemes have the benefit of a clear, usually measurable purpose, which cannot happen with informal mentoring. Indeed, informal mentoring may frequently work against business objectives. I have encountered numerous cases where the informal mentoring networks have placed malleable young recruits in the hands of people who represent the culture as it used to be rather than the culture top management is trying to build. Within a formal scheme it is possible to ensure that mentees are exposed to mentors who represent the organisation's current values and ways of thinking.

Ideally, of course, we should be able to train every manager and professional within a company in the skills of mentoring and let people find each other. In practice it will never be that easy. Even if every manager were capable of being an effective mentor, you would still need some system to help learners find the mentor best suited to their needs at the time. And why should top management invest in such training or in encouraging people to spend valuable time in mentoring if there is no means of assessing whether it is doing any good?

It is difficult to construct a tenable argument against the pragmatic approach of seeking to achieve a balance between control, through a scheme framework, and autonomy, through letting each relationship establish its own ways of working. Where an organisation decides to place that balance depends on circumstances and culture, but Table 7 gives an indication of the kind of choices that can be made.

This capacity for organising mentoring and the practical benefits of doing so are another factor that make mentoring qualitatively different from other forms of helping others to learn. However, as we shall examine in the next chapter, it is now becoming increasingly common for organisations to develop schemes that support mentoring by training managers in some or all of the other 'helping to learn' roles – in particular, coaching.

Table 7

FORMAL v INFORMAL MENTORING: THE SPECTRUM OF CONTROL

Measurement	For programme review	For benefit of programme and individuals	For benefit of mentor and mentee	No measurement
Recording	Activity logs open to HR	Activity logs kept by mentor/mentee	Activity logs used as discussion triggers	No activity logs
Agenda	Formal, agreed in advance	Formal, agreed on the spot	Informal, agreed on the spot	No agenda: random discussion
Programme management	Official scheme co-ordinator	Organised peer support group	*Ad hoc* support for mentors and mentees	No support for mentors or mentees

Those organisations that report the greatest benefits from mentoring share a number of common characteristics in their schemes. They normally include:

☐ a clear definition of scheme purpose

☐ a realistic understanding of how the development climate and culture of the organisation will support or hinder mentoring behaviours

☐ a set of measurements to assess whether the scheme is helping to achieve the purpose, and to ensure that each relationship is on course

☐ a well-thought-through method of selecting mentors and mentees, and clear criteria of what makes a good mentor

☐ a system to manage relationships that do not work out

☐ relevant initial training of both mentors and mentees plus, in many cases, training for key third parties, such as mentees' line managers

☐ a scheme co-ordinator, with the skills to troubleshoot as necessary

☐ public support from top management (especially if they are willing to talk openly about the value they gain from their own mentoring)

Table 8

THE SPECTRUM OF MENTORING RELATIONSHIPS

Organisation selects/pairs mentees and mentor	Mentor selects mentee with help from HR	Mentee selects mentor (with help from HR) from a panel of well-trained mentors	FORMAL
Organisation develops and trains pool of mentors and encourages relationships to happen	Mentor makes interest known to mentee	Mentee informs HR of selection; approaches mentor	SEMI-FORMAL
Organisation tolerates *ad hoc* mentoring	Mentor 'adopts' mentee. Gradual evolution of relationship	Mentee makes interest known to mentor. Gradual evolution of relationship	INFORMAL
Control by organisation	Control by mentor	Control by mentee	

☐ continued support and development of the mentors, typically through opportunities to continue to meet, discuss and share experience.

Where schemes have failed, they have always lacked several of these characteristics.

Keeping the balance between bureaucracy and autonomy is critical to the scheme design and to the co-ordinator's role. Formal and informal mentoring are not necessarily discrete activities: they are parts of the spectrum determined by where the focus of control lies, as Table 8 describes.

Managing the mentoring relationship

Mentoring relationships also seem to work best when they have a clear purpose. The clearer the transition the learner is aiming for – whether it is a change in confidence, situation or competence – the easier it is for both mentor and mentee to make effective use of reflective space. Without some sense of shared goals, mentor and mentee may struggle to achieve commitment to the relationship, especially if they are not people who would instinctively become friends.

Figure 23
MATCHING MENTOR WITH MENTEE

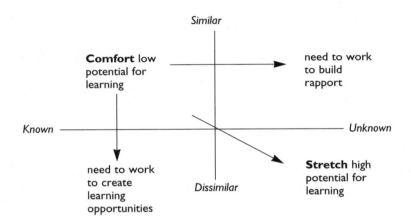

While successful mentoring relationships will typically result in professional friendship, the quality and quantity of learning that takes place, on both sides, is usually greater if the two people are not instinctive soul-mates. The reasoning behind this observation, which is well-supported by practical experience, is illustrated in Figure 23.

Where the learner is lacking in confidence, needing reassurance or simply relatively immature (say, a young graduate), it may help to be matched with a mentor who is fairly similar in interests, personality, discipline and background. In most cases this will result in rapid establishment of rapport – particularly valuable if the objective is to help the young graduate fit in and feel valued. If the goal is to stimulate a high level of learning, however, the two people may simply be too similar; some grit is needed in the oyster.

At the opposite extreme, where the two people are radically different in their personality and experience, the potential for learning will be very high but it will require relatively mature individuals to take advantage of it. Some very effective individual mentees have sought out over their careers successively more challenging relationships, recognising the value of exposing themselves to discomfort and discontinuity. They feel relatively secure in doing so because they have progresively gained confidence in their ability to handle different perspectives and because they have strong trust in the mentors' goodwill towards them.

As the relationship develops, the initial purpose may become superseded by another, or a succession of new goals. The mentor needs to have the flexibility to respond to each of these changes as they occur and to encourage the mentee to seek out new learning goals and opportunities.

Clarity of purpose makes it easier to have clear expectations about the benefits the learner will gain from the relationship and to assess from time to time how the learner is progressing towards his or her goals. But it is also important to bring the mentor's expectations into the open, both in terms of the behaviours that each party will show to the other and in terms of benefits to the mentor. Experience suggests that this discussion rarely takes place unless it is built into mentor training (or ideally mentee training too) as an important part of the relationship management process.

The concept of a mentoring contract occurs frequently in the literature on schemes, but what is meant by the term varies widely, from precise details of the learning goals, expected behaviours and relationship boundaries, to a broad understanding. Again, practical experience suggests that the degree of formality about the mentoring contract should depend on the organisational culture and the preferences of the mentoring pair. In an experiment some years ago with 100 mentoring pairs, each pair was given the option of using an extensive kit of guidelines, contract templates and other documentation. Some used the paperwork extensively, some referred to it occasionally for guidance, and some ignored it altogether after an initial read-through to gather the principles. As the relationships progressed, there appeared to be no appreciable difference in success rate between these three groups: the level of bureaucracy people felt most comfortable with was generally the 'right' level for their relationship.

The minimum requirement, however, is that mentor and mentee should discuss the issues of relationship purpose and relationship management sufficiently to acquire a shared understanding of them. The most common topics for this discussion are:

- ☐ What do we expect to learn from each other?
- ☐ What are our responsibilities towards each other? What are the limits?
- ☐ What responsibilities do we owe to others as a result of this relationship – eg
  - – to line managers
  - – to peers
  - – to the HR function?
- ☐ Where and how often shall we meet? For how long?
- ☐ What limits (if any) are there on confidentiality?
- ☐ When and how shall we check this relationship is 'right' for both of us?
- ☐ Is there anything either of us definitely does not want to talk about?
- ☐ Are we agreed that openness and trust are essential? How shall we ensure they happen?
- ☐ Are we both willing to give honest and timely feedback (eg to be a critical friend)?
- ☐ What are we prepared to tell others about our discussions?
- ☐ How formal or informal do we want our meetings to be?
- ☐ How shall we measure progress?
- ☐ How shall we manage the various transitions, especially at the end of the formal relationship?
- ☐ To what extent are we prepared to share networks?

Like purpose, the 'contract' terms will evolve with the relationship. It is commonplace for one party or both to place quite narrow limits on how far the pair will delve into non-work issues, for example. Yet as trust develops, the boundaries on discussion tend to soften or fold completely.

If the relationship does not work out (even in the best of schemes, the chemistry may simply not be right), there has to be a mechanism for confronting the issues. Neither mentor nor mentee may be willing to say 'Look, this isn't working, is it?' for fear of embarrassment, letting the other person down, or even fear of retribution. The concept of 'no-fault divorce' is helpful here. Essentially, mentor and mentee are expected to engage in a discussion about whether they are suited to each other after the first two or three meetings, at the latest. Both sides need to understand the importance of responding honestly and openly, and that it is better to deal with the issues now, when relatively little face will be lost by admitting the relationship will not work, than to be locked into a relationship that neither will find fulfilling.

The fact that a relationship did not gel at one point in the learner's progress does not mean that the same person will not have potential as a mentor for his or her future needs. Where the mismatch concerns style or relevance of experience (as opposed to trust), there is often a possibility of reinstating it at a later date. The case-study below illustrates just such a situation.

Case-study

THE RELUCTANT MENTEE

John and Roger were assigned to each other under a graduate entry scheme in a large UK-based multinational. This was John's first job after university and he was having trouble adapting to the very different lifestyle of the organisation. John found Roger, who was head of another department of 200 people, to be unsympathetic, overcritical and overwhelming.

John spoke to the personnel department about his reservations. A few days later he received a note from Roger suggesting four names of other, more junior managers he should contact, to choose his own mentor. He hit it off so well with Mary, the first on the list, that he did not talk to any of the others.

Two years later he had outgrown Mary's help and felt he was making a useful contribution to the company. He applied to join a high-profile project team, only to be dismayed when he discovered that Roger was on the selection panel.

The interview was every bit as tough as he expected, but to his surprise he enjoyed the experience. Even more to his surprise Roger recommended his inclusion on the team. After working with Roger for a few months, John realised that he had matured to the point where Roger's challenging style was exactly what he needed. When the project ended, the two became mentor and mentee without anyone raising the subject. 'It just seemed the natural thing to do,' said John.

Among the most obvious clues as to whether a relationship is working is whether and how often people meet. There are, of course, no hard and fast rules about this, but a good guideline is that the pair should meet formally often enough to create a real relationship, yet not so often that they develop dependency.

The mentoring meeting itself can cover a wide variety of topics concerning both work and personal lives. The mentor needs to be sensitive about when to be a bit more directive or nurturing and when the learner has the confidence to take greater charge of the relationship. Both need to focus on the goal of making the learner completely independent of the mentor.

The approach – which effective mentors almost universally adopt – is illustrated in Figure 24. First they create a relaxed yet professional atmosphere in which both parties can use the rapport they have already developed. Next they encourage the mentee to explain the issue for discussion, as he or she sees it. If the relationship is well established, the mentee will already have given some thought (devoted some personal reflective space to) the issue.

An ineffective mentor might jump in here with advice or solutions. But the effective mentor holds fire. First, he or she seeks clarification. How much of what the mentee is saying is fact and how much assumption? What was the mentee feeling at the time? Why is it so important? And so on.

Then the mentor probes more deeply, testing the assumptions and reasoning behind what has been said. Is it logical? Is it really an isolated issue or part of a larger pattern? He or she then encourages a typical short but broader discussion that opens the issue to other perspectives. How would the mentee perceive it if he or she was an outsider? What alternative explanations might there be?

Only at the end of this stage of the discussion does the mentor make significant use of his or her own experience as a stepping-stone to solutions. (He or she may well indicate similar experience to empathise, but not in detail – this is still the mentee's show!) Again, the temptation is to tell old war stories, but effective mentors resist. Rather, they selectively use examples to show that the issue is not unique to the mentee, and that there is more than one way of tackling it. They are careful not to suggest that what worked for them will necessarily work for the mentee. (This is not about trans-ferring my experience so much as helping you use my experi-ence to develop your own approaches.) Some of the deepest learning for the mentor comes out of exposing his or her experience for critical analysis in this way.

At this point comes a fundamental shift in the nature of the discussion, as it moves from data-gathering and analysis to problem-solving. The first, vital, step here is to reassure learn-ers, building their confidence that they can tackle the issue and helping them to vision the benefits of doing so. The next is to lay out the alternative solutions and evaluate them in terms of feasibility, likelihood of success, degree of effort required, general comfort about each approach, and so on. (Discomfort with an apparently potent solution may trigger a further round of probing discussion.) Once a way forward has been selected, the question becomes 'What will each of us do about this?' The bulk of the responsibility for action must rest with the mentee, but the mentor may agree to make an intro-duction, find some relevant background reading or provide some form of template from an experience elsewhere.

If the learner does not wish to make a decision right now about the action to be taken, the mentor should respect that wish. It is not the mentor's role to force an agreement. Indeed, my experience is that the outcome – for that meeting, at least – is often an understanding that the mentee will go away to think more deeply about the alternatives and gather more evaluative data, making the decision back in his or her own personal reflective space.

Finally, mentor and mentee review what has been dis-cussed. Here, once again, many mentors blow it by suddenly snatching back ownership of the problem, summarising the dialogue and checking that the learner agrees. Effective men-tors recognise how disempowering that would be and encour-age the learner to summarise instead.

They then come to an agreement on whether any of the issues should be carried over to the next meeting, or whether the mentee would like to bring up a particular topic next time. The purpose of doing so is not to check on the mentee but to enable both parties to prepare their thoughts before-hand.

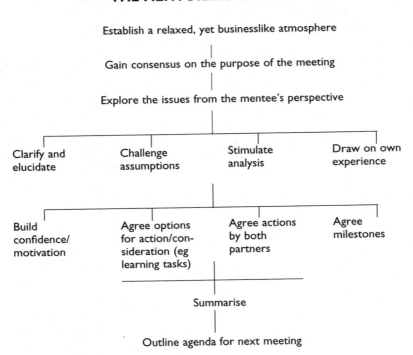

Figure 24
THE MENTORING MEETING

Establish a relaxed, yet businesslike atmosphere

Gain consensus on the purpose of the meeting

Explore the issues from the mentee's perspective

| Clarify and elucidate | Challenge assumptions | Stimulate analysis | Draw on own experience |

| Build confidence/ motivation | Agree options for action/con- sideration (eg learning tasks) | Agree actions by both partners | Agree milestones |

Summarise

Outline agenda for next meeting

The consistency, with which effective mentors instinctively follow this broad pattern of dialogue, is remarkable.

What goes wrong with mentoring programmes?

Experience with literally hundreds of successful and unsuccessful mentoring schemes reveals a number of common causes of problems. Among them are:

□ failure to involve the line manager
□ poor planning and preparation.

Failure to involve the line manager

The line manager has the capacity to make or break the relationship. If that person is suspicious or resentful, it is hardly surprising if he or she tries to discourage it. Companies such as BP Chemicals help overcome line-manager resistance by asking the manager to introduce any graduate in his or her care to the mentor. Other companies involve the line managers in the design and review of the programme.

Poor planning and preparation

The classic case of poor planning for a mentoring scheme is the retail chain that sent out to every one of its managers in its several hundred stores a long memo telling them that henceforth they were mentors. The complete absence of any support, other than a few scrappy notes in the memo about what mentors do, and the lack of any follow-up not only ensured that virtually none of the 2,000 managers took the role seriously but prevented the introduction of an effective mentoring scheme for years afterwards.

The planning process needs to consider a wide range of issues, each of which will have an impact on the success or otherwise of the initiative. Among them are:

- Do we want to unleash a company-wide scheme with maximum publicity or start small with a closely monitored pilot? (The former is often most applicable when mentoring is seen as part of a major, rapidly implemented, hard-driven programme of culture change; the latter when change is intended to take place incrementally or when the organisation has a strong reserve of cynicism towards 'soft' management issues.)
- Have we got sufficient backing and commitment from top management?
- What target groups should be given priority? There will not be enough mentors to provide one for everybody, at least at the start, so it is essential to identify who has first option, and why.

How do the target groups feel about it? When one multinational company first considered introducing a mentoring scheme to help women move into middle and senior management positions, it prudently gathered a large cross-section of the women to gain their views. It soon became clear that –

contrary to the expectations of the human resource department – there was little interest in establishing a special scheme just for women, because this could be seen as creating yet another ghetto. Instead, the women wanted a broader mentoring scheme for both men and women, which they could be encouraged and supported in joining.

What goes wrong with mentoring relationships?

The reasons are of course many and varied, but the most common include:

- failure to establish rapport
- under- or overmanagement
- poor objective-setting
- time pressures
- geographical separation
- problems from other people
- breach of confidence.

Failure to establish rapport

If rapport does not happen fairly early on, in the first few meetings, it probably will not happen at all – at least, not this time around. Hence the need for the 'no-fault divorce clause' in every relationship. It is not essential that the two like each other: in some of the most effective mentoring relationships, the mentor may admit privately that he or she finds the mentee boorish, arrogant, cold, or in some other wise difficult to empathise with. More important is the capacity of the pair to establish mutual trust. If one or both is constantly guarding his or her words, then there is no real opportunity to delve deep into the mentee's issues, nor to tap the mentor's most significant reservoirs of experience.

Sometimes the mentor can make a breakthrough by demonstrating greater trust than he or she actually feels (a sort of 'If I show you mine, will you show me yours?'), deliberately exposing part of the private self to encourage the mentee. It typically requires great maturity (or near-suicidal immaturity!) to do so, however.

Under- or overmanagement

The temptation to bureaucratise the relationship, relying on forms and templates, can take away all the life and spontaneity, whether the initiative in doing so comes from the mentor, the mentee, or both. On the other hand, someone has to make sure that the meetings happen, that issues are brought forward from one meeting to the next, and that the relationship is sufficiently purposeful. Getting the balance right comes with practice, but experience of both suggests mentor and mentee should err on the side of avoiding being too demanding, or too controlling.

Poor objective-setting

Especially where mentor and mentee establish immediate rapport, there is a potential to spend the time enjoying each other's companionship, congratulating each other on the 'rightness' of their views – and missing the important issues, because both are equally blind to them. The move from rapport-building to direction-setting needs to take place very early on in the relationship. The nature of the transition that the mentee wants to make should be identified firmly and clearly, along with how the mentor will help the mentee achieve it. The relationship objectives can change with circumstances, of course, but the likelihood of significant learning outcomes is minimal if both parties are not focused on clear relationship goals.

Time pressures

Virtually every mentor and mentee complains about the difficulty of finding time for the relationship. However, in successful relationships people find the time because they want to. Almost invariably, whenever people blame time pressures for not meeting, it is an excuse for another problem within the relationship itself.

Geographical separation

This is a real issue but, again, some pairs turn it to advantage. Because it is more disruptive to cancel a meeting that requires a journey than one held with someone in the same building, mentoring pairs separated by distance often meet more frequently and regularly than those very close together. What the former lack, however, is the relationship-reinforcing benefit of *ad hoc* discussions and casual 'coffee-machine' meetings that may take place naturally in the same location. Telephone calls and e-mail provide something of a substitute, and there is some evidence to suggest that mentees think about the issues more deeply when using these media than when they are taking advantage of a chance meeting or drop-in chat.

Problems from other people

The most commonly reported problems with other people concern either the mentee's line manager or his or her peers. The line manager may feel resentful at the opportunities extended to the learner if his or her own career never received such support. (I have actually had a potential mentor say openly, 'I didn't have any of this when I joined the company, so I don't see why these graduates should be getting such privileges now.') The line manager may also be concerned over whether the mentor and mentee are discussing him or her, and in what terms – especially if the mentor is more senior than the line manager. And that manager may resent any real or imagined 'interference' by the mentor in his or her department, especially if the mentee seeks and accepts advice contrary to that given by the line manager.

Part of the solution here lies in making sure that the mentoring relationship does not move too far into the sponsorship style. But equally, the more the line manager can be involved as a partner in the mentee's learning net, the less the need or opportunity for concern.

Peers may express resentment at the special treatment given to the mentee if they do not also have the opportunity to acquire a mentor. The wider the range of development alternatives the organisation offers, the less the problem. However, the mentee has to exercise restraint in how he or she presents the relationship. Although it would be difficult and perhaps counter-productive (and, hopefully, counter-cultural) deliberately to hide the relationship, neither should they flaunt it. (One delegate at a European Mentoring Centre

Conference referred to such insensitive behaviour as 'treating the mentor as a fashion accessory'.)

Confidentiality

Actually, this is not a common problem at all, simply because most people are aware of the consequences of breaking confidence – but it is always an issue of concern to novice mentors or mentees. The biggest dangers come from the mentor breaching *other people's* confidences – that is, telling the mentee information about other people to which they would not otherwise be privy. Leakages of this kind can be disastrous, both for the relationship and for mentoring within the whole organisation.

Power in the mentoring relationship

Developmental mentoring works best when the overt differences in power and influence between the mentor and mentee are 'parked' so that the two can concentrate on learning issues. Relatively little is known about the mechanisms mentors use to park power – there have been no specific studies on the topic, to my knowledge – but some of the most obvious include:

☐ selecting a neutral environment (not the mentor's office)

☐ removing any kind of power differential in where and how people sit

☐ encouraging the learner to challenge the mentor's views and statements

☐ acknowledging the two-way nature of the learning.

Appendix 1 (at the end of the book) provides a discussion of power issues in greater depth.

The special case of mentoring at the top

There are not many situations in which the mentor has to come from outside, but the nearer you get to the top, the more difficult it becomes to find someone with whom you can be fully open. Moreover, because learning at the top has to emphasise breadth rather than depth, people within the company may simply be too similar in their experience.

A few companies, such as T&N, have experimented with peer-mentoring among executive directors of subsidiary boards. But most of the rapidly increasing number of executive development alliances involve some form of outsider. In some cases the outsider acts as a short-term coach, focusing on particular skills needs or behaviour modification. In others, the executive develops a relationship with an 'elder statesman' – a very experienced director, who is able to give advice and introductions. This kind of relationship may last several decades.

The developmental mentor for executives is a somewhat different beast, however. Increasingly, this person is a professional mentor, although he or she may still maintain an active involvement in real businesses. Such mentors' skills of coaching, counselling, advising and networking will be several steps higher than the norm. They will have very good practical knowledge of business realities as well as good skills in behaviour development. Their store of relevant business, strategic and behavioural models – and their ability to generate others on the spot – allows them to help executives explore the context of both personal and business issues.

The check-list below was designed to help HR directors think through how they select and use professional mentors.

Check-list for HR directors: using professional mentors

Current best practice suggests:

□ Start small. Encourage two or three executives to seek mentors to begin with – people who have the capacity to become champions of the process if it works for them. Ideal candidates for professional mentoring are often people who have just taken on, or will soon take on, a major new challenge; for coaching, someone for whom a particular behavioural issue is an impediment to performance/promotion.

□ Spend time talking through with the executive what he or she expects from the relationship and how he or she will manage it. Use this discussion to help the executive to think through what kind of mentor he or she will most benefit from/enjoy. (These may not be the same.)

□ Examine the track record of any provider – both the

individual mentor and the organisation. Does he or she have the skills and experience required for *this* executive's needs?

□ Build into the arrangement an option to change mentor at any stage – either because the relationship is not working or because the executive's needs have changed.

□ Once you have some examples of effective executive-level mentoring, consider using these people as ambassadors to legitimise and promote the value of mentoring at other levels of the organisation, using in-house mentors. Create an expectation that executive mentors will become mentors in their turn.

The integrative role of mentoring

Whichever level mentoring is practised at – from the basic to the professional – it will always draw on a range of other developmental or career management behaviours. It will always require great flexibility of style and approach by the mentor. And it should always support rather than replace other forms of learning.

For all these reasons, it seems logical to think of mentoring as a kind of second-level or higher skill than, say, coaching or counselling, and that people should be trained as mentors only after they have demonstrated their capability in one or more of the constituent skills. The resulting breadth of role management should have a significant positive effect on the original skill. But there is an alternative, opposite argument that says that mentoring should be the starting-point for developing coaching and counselling skills. The reasoning is that however flawed the person's approach is, mentoring is such an instinctive skill that he or she can at least make a stab at it, given some basic training.

In practice, it probably does not matter whether mentoring sits on top of the 'helping to learn' web or below it. It still provides the integrative rational for a portfolio of helping approaches that will cover most of the needs of the people within an organisation. Giving people the skills to practise mentoring behaviours can only be beneficial, to them and to the organisation.

Given the potential for two people simply not to get on

with each other, it is remarkable how many mentoring relationships work, informally and formally. Compared with, say, the TV programme *Blind Date*, the hit rate is astoundingly high. But even where everything seems to be right – both mentor and mentee trained, sensitive matching, with both parties exercising some degree of choice, and a clear scheme purpose – the relationship can go badly wrong, as we have seen.

Conclusion

Mentoring truly is the integrating role, because it draws so heavily on the behaviours and intent of the other roles. The keys to being an effective mentor are:

- knowing when and how to move from one role to another across the dimensions of directivity and mentee need
- having the sensitivity to recognise the boundaries of the role and being able to help the mentee seek alternative, additional help
- managing one's own learning and self awareness – recognising the relationship as a journey for two people
- always remembering that the journey is towards empowerment, and acting accordingly.

The more capable the mentor is in the constituent roles of coach, counsellor, guardian and networker/facilitator, the easier all these elements of effective mentoring become.

7 LEARNING ALLIANCES WITHIN THE DEVELOPMENT FRAMEWORK

The styles and goals of mentoring

The framework outlined so far in this book is a logical and practical way of linking the various one-to-one developmental roles. Thousands of managers in recent years have found in it a readily understandable and easily applicable template for managing their one-to-one helping relationships at work – both giving and receiving. In this concluding chapter it is useful to review how all five roles and their component styles fit together. A swift glance at Figure 25 reveals a symmetry that is broken only in the counselling box. (Remember how, at the beginning, we pointed out that counselling was a different form of helping to learn?) Counselling reflects the geometry of the others because it has both an intrinsic and an extrinsic focus. But it also aligns against the intellectual/emotional need dimension of the main framework in its mutual objectives of helping people both cope and grow.

So where and how does mentoring fit in? The shaded boxes represent the styles all effective mentors use – the core content of the mentoring role. The needs of the mentee, the context of any formal mentoring scheme and the extent of the mentor's skills base will determine which other styles may be appropriate to adopt, according to circumstance. Some are highly unlikely. For example, in adopting the assessor style a mentor would almost certainly be taking him- or herself out of role, with high potential to damage the relationship. Taking on a sponsoring style would not normally be regarded as appropriate in a north European organisation.

In the counselling box, all of the styles might be appropriate

Figure 25
THOSE HELPING STYLES IN FULL

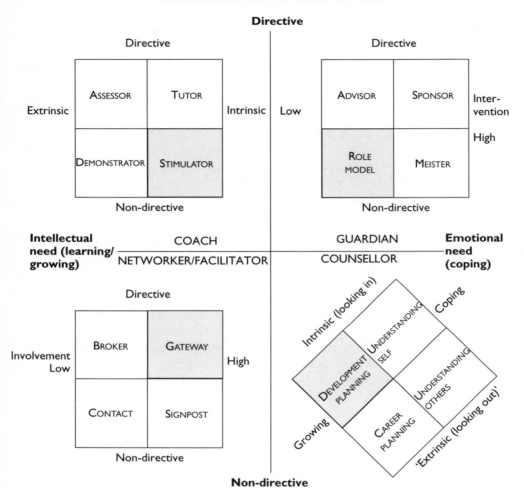

but the mentor needs to watch out for the *scope* of the issues identified. When issues move away from personal development and into psychological problems, warning bells should ring very loudly. As emphasised in the chapter on mentoring, the fundamental skill of the mentor is the sensitivity to recognise which style to adopt and where the many boundaries lie.

I have played all these roles and used all the styles over

Figure 26
RESPONSIBILITIES IN DEVELOPMENT

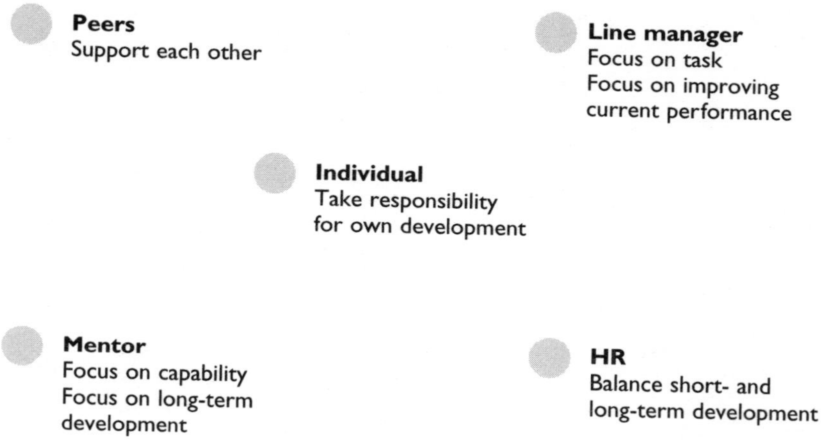

Peers
Support each other

Line manager
Focus on task
Focus on improving
current performance

Individual
Take responsibility
for own development

Mentor
Focus on capability
Focus on long-term
development

HR
Balance short- and
long-term development

the years and I recognise that I am innately far more comfortable in some than in others. As a learner, therefore, I sometimes actively seek opportunities to practise in some of those less comfortable areas. By doing so, not only do I make interesting discoveries about myself but I enhance my overall style sensitivity. The moment I forget that this is a learning journey for me, too, I begin to lose some of my edge as a developer.

On its own, however, the framework is simply intellectually interesting. But, the framework gains its real impact as an operating tool only when it is clearly linked to the organisation's task and learning goals.

Making that link requires several elements. Firstly, it requires some kind of policy or statement of expectations about people's responsibilities for developing themselves and others. Figure 26 sets out one such policy.

If everyone is clear about their responsibilities, it legitimises a whole range of helping relationships, both for the learners and for the sources of help.

Secondly, the link requires clear learning goals at individual, team and organisation level. These may take the form of

Figure 27
A PERSONAL DEVELOPMENT PLANNING NET

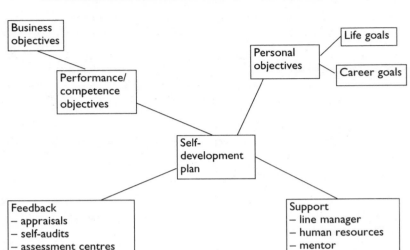

competencies or be the outcome of strategic processes that have identified critical development needs across the organisation and/or in specific areas. The more people can tie in their personal ambitions to organisational learning goals, the easier it is to achieve both.

Effective personal development plans (PDPs) draw on a wide variety of sources of information and have a holistic view of development (see figure 27). They recognise that people who aim to achieve in only one sphere of their lives typically limit what they can achieve in all spheres. It is important to achieve a balance of objectives: business/performance, career and non-career (family, leisure, health, general intellectual development, and so on); a balance and variety of sources of feedback; and a balance and variety of sources of support and learning.

Thirdly, it requires some kind of planning mechanism for learning. In theory, PDPs should cater for much of this need, but in practice they often fail to deliver significant motivation for learning. To benefit both the individual and the organisation, PDPs need to:

- ❑ balance both short-term (task) and long-term (capability) goals
- ❑ balance job and career objectives against goals in other life-streams (family, physical fitness, leisure, self-fulfilment, and so on)
- ❑ set clear and measurable milestones for achievement
- ❑ draw on frequent feedback to assess progress
- ❑ define actual and potential sources of help and support
- ❑ allow for both planned and serendipitous learning
- ❑ mesh closely with the team development plan (assuming there is one), which should in turn be aligned with broader organisation learning goals.

Few PDP processes deliver on even half of these criteria. The technology to support an integrated system of this kind is readily available. What is often lacking is the will to engage in such clarity and to unleash widespread demand from people in the organisation for developmental support. Many organisations are simply not ready to accept an environment where a high proportion of employees insist on taking regular, quality, reflective time for themselves, let alone insist that managers partake with them! The implications for how managers spend their time are enormous: how many managers now spend even a quarter of their time in developmental activities?

Yet it is precisely this kind of fudge that prevents the direct link between individual learning and organisational learning. Development alliances provide a way of bridging the gap, at least in part. The more they can be linked into a broader development framework, the more effectively they will do so.

Managing the development framework

Experience of a wide variety of coaching, mentoring and self-development schemes suggests that development frameworks work best when they fulfil a number of criteria:

- ❑ There is a clear organisational purpose.
- ❑ There have to be appropriate resources.
- ❑ The development climate must be transparent.
- ❑ Development career paths can be an added incentive for both learners and helpers.

- ☐ Top management must set the example.
- ☐ The training structure ensures that all development roles are well supported.
- ☐ The more extensive the use of learning alliances, the greater is the need for some kind of development resource base.
- ☐ What gets measures gets done.

There is a clear organisational purpose

Development, whether individual or organisational has to be for a purpose. It might be to improve the organisation's capacity to respond flexibly to external change, to provide succession-planning for key posts, or to improve retention of skilled employees. Whatever the reason, the more clearly it is articulated and understood by learners, helpers and other influencers, the more likely people are to commit themselves to the goals. If, in addition, it is possible to demonstrate a contribution to the bottom line through achieving the goals, the whole process receives an added impetus.

There have to be appropriate resources

The assumption that coaching and mentoring are cheap methods of development is questionable at best. When off-line mentoring works well, for example, it typically increases the demands the mentee makes upon his or her line manager. The mentor, too, may come under pressure from direct reports, who quite rightly want to know how he or she can afford to give so much more quality time to someone outside the department than to them. The more conscious the mentees become of development opportunities around them, the more access they are likely to seek to external courses, distance learning materials, and so on. Similarly, the more effective the line manager becomes as coach or facilitator of learning, the more learning resources the team is likely to require.

Somehow the organisation has to anticipate and meet this demand without vast increases in budget while containing people's instinct to spend more and more time off the job. Failure to manage these expectations will lead to disillusionment and a fading of commitment as people perceive that the organisation is not really serious. Part of the answer is to push back the responsibility onto the team and the individual – but this can work only if there are sufficient self-help resources and if people know how to access them. The HR function has a major marketing task on its hands!

The development climate must be transparent

Understanding the barriers and drivers to development within the organisation helps considerably in planning the introduction of development alliances. HR needs to carry out detailed internal market research among all the key audiences involved: top management, as the role models and budget providers; managers in general, as the people who have to make the time available; various groups of learners; and the HR team itself.

Sometimes simple changes can make a major difference. For example, one organisation found that its rigid system of charging time was freezing out development, because people were under great pressure to meet delivery targets first. Creating an accounting line for development time changed people's attitudes and behaviour almost overnight.

Development career paths as incentive for learners and helpers

As developing talent becomes increasingly recognised to be a core skill for managers, there will be a growing demand from managers themselves for some form of recognition of their competence as developers. The NVQ (National Vocational Qualification) and MCI (Management Charter Initiative) systems may go some way towards meeting that demand in the UK, but are unlikely to be enough on their own. Some companies are now considering the possibilities in creating explicit patterns of developer development. One possible approach is shown in Figure 28.

In this progression, a graduate recruit (say) might receive initial help on induction from a 'buddy' – someone at a similar level but who has been around long enough to know the ropes. As the graduate's immediate skills needs become clear, he or she is assigned a coach (typically the line manager or someone else in the team). The coach's role is then

Figure 28
A CAREER PATH FOR DEVELOPERS

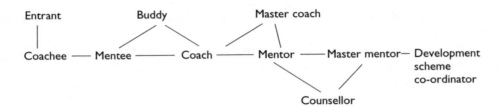

supplemented by the broader attentions of a mentor, who will help the learner look beyond the immediate task and job.

By this time, the learner is probably ready to act as a buddy in turn. As the learner gains in skill and experience, he or she can take over some basic coaching of newcomers, and this coaching competence will grow as that individual goes on to become a supervisor or manager. With evidence of effective coaching, the person can apply (or be talent-spotted through the appraisal system) to train as a mentor and/or a master coach.

The master coach is, in essence, a coach to less experienced coaches – a role model, guide and troubleshooter outside the HR function. In the same fashion, effective mentors who have several years' experience with a number of mentees may become master mentors, looking after a group of less experienced mentors. To reach that level, they will want to acquire deeper skills and/or qualifications both in coaching and in counselling that they can apply to the role.

Finally, some master mentors may wish to make a career shift – temporary or permanent – away from the line and into the HR stream. The role of development scheme co-ordinator, overseeing the management and integration of a variety of one-to-one and small-group learning processes in the workplace (as opposed to in the classroom), is likely to become a valuable stepping-stone for ambitious people-oriented managers with their eye on the executive suite.

Top management must set the example
One of the most successful mentoring schemes in recent

years has been within a public-sector organisation that had a broadly hostile climate towards informal development. Top management was determined to change the culture and recognised that their own behaviour was critical in that process. Many of the most senior managers volunteered to be mentors themselves: some sought mentors. But the most influential of all was the chief executive, who attended virtually every training course for mentors and mentees in order to talk about his own experiences as a mentee. He spoke of the kind of help he sought and received from his mentor, and how he had made use of the relationship to gain a different perspective on issues that were worrying him. The result was not only to legitimise the development alliance as an acceptable use of working time, but also to boost other learning activities.

One of the big problems for top managers is that they often switch off to learning as they rise in the hierarchy. They may even regress in learning maturity, becoming narrower and narrower in their choice of learning opportunities. Many directors, for example, limit their learning to a small amount of reading, what they pick up from internal meetings, or attending the occasional conference (although they may only dip in and out as a speaker rather than as a participant). At the next layer down, senior managers may feel free to attend executive-level courses at the top business schools but still avoid most internal training. 'It's too exposed,' said one to me recently. 'You have to be constantly on the watch so that you don't get too much into the spirit of things and reveal things that aren't appropriate for the other participants to know.' He might also have added that he was afraid of being made to look foolish for being less knowledgeable than participants from lower grades.

Involving top management as development leaders and role models can have huge benefits for them too. Any form of development alliance outside US-style sponsorship involves some element of learning by discussion for the helper, if he or she has the skill to draw issues out of the learner and explore them in depth. Simply training top managers as coaches or mentors, for example, enables them to create an environment in which they can learn without having to admit to it. Providing top management coaches and/or mentors with a continuing support group, where they help each other develop their skills, also helps them broaden out their learning nets. In some cases top managers develop such increased confidence in their ability to continue learning – and awareness of the importance of doing so – that they establish very wide learning nets and share their personal learning needs with other people, including both peers and direct reports.

(An aside here: switching top managers on to the symbolic importance of their example as continuous learners is a critical part of developing the learning organisation. Among the signs of the organisation's learning maturity are:

☐ Top managers share the key points from their PDPs with a wide audience in the organisation.

☐ Top managers seek frequent feedback about their behaviour.

☐ Top managers spend a lot of time 'learning by listening' – to employees, customers – anyone with a legitimate view of the business.

☐ The company runs courses, with mixed levels of participants, that all executives, including the CEO, must join. For example, several companies insist that all new recruits spend several days being immersed in the company values.

☐ Top managers spend at least 10 per cent of their time developing themselves, 20 per cent developing others.)

The training structure supports all development roles

For a variety of largely obvious reasons, learning alliances work best when all the parties involved understand their roles and the skills needed, and when they have an opportunity to reflect on and improve those skills. A rough estimate is that alliances put together without any training (issuing a few guidance notes does not count as training!) will deliver meaningful results for one or both parties in perhaps three out of ten relationships. If the helper is well trained, the success rate rises to around seven out of ten. If the learner is also trained, both parties are likely to record significant benefits in nine out of ten relationships. If third parties (such as the line manager of a mentee) are also trained to support the relationship, the success rate may be even higher.

Training for learning alliances has to address both behavioural skills and relationship management skills in order to be really effective. Because the variety of situations that the learner might bring to the table is so large, the skills input has to be generic. So the participants may all need additional support to maintain the continuous improvement of their skills and to ensure that new situations can be built into the personal and organisational repertoire.

Both helpers and learners in learning alliances need to meet within their own group on a regular basis to seek and exchange learning from their peers. The benefits of these sessions (which counsellors refer to as supervision) can often be greater if they are facilitated or chaired by someone who is not part of the group. In my experience, as the group learns to 'look after its own' the facilitator's role gradually becomes less and less proactive, evolving into one composed mostly of keeping the group on track and linking the group with other, external sources of learning they may not be aware of.

The development resource base

The more extensive the use of learning alliances, the greater is the need for some kind of development resource base. First and foremost there has to be an HR professional who takes on the role of co-ordinator of development alliances. This person must be knowledgeable about all areas of one-to-one development and have good project-management skills. Among his or key responsibilities are:

☐ promoting the concept of development alliances in general (and/or specific types of alliance in particular)

☐ assessing and selecting target groups with line managers, where appropriate

☐ identifying potential participants (or encouraging them to come forward)

☐ providing appropriate training and continuous support

☐ managing the matching process, where appropriate

☐ providing measurement and monitoring – in particular, providing feedback on the scheme as a whole to key stakeholders such as participants and top management

☐ troubleshooting, as necessary.

The basic computer software now exists[1] to help such co-ordinators maintain a database of managers and others who can contribute as partners in development alliances. Typical data to include would be:

- skills and aptitudes (learner and helper)
- general track record as a developer of others (helper)
- duration and outcome of previous alliances the person has been involved in; any comments/assessment by previous alliance partners (helper and learner)
- nature and duration of formal training received as a people developer (helper)
- demographic data – eg age, gender, where located, mobility (helper and learner)
- special interests (helper and learner).

Software will also gradually become available that enables people to define and manage their own learning nets and to share portions of their learning nets with others electronically.

It is also important for both parties in the learning alliance to have rapid access to learning materials – for example, within a learning resource centre.

What gets measured gets done

Learning alliances that work best typically begin with a clear understanding of what the participants want to achieve, both individually and jointly (the relationship objectives) *and* with a clear understanding of what the organisation expects to achieve (the scheme objectives). In theory, at least, the more all these sets of objectives are aligned, the greater the impetus behind the relationship will be.

Progress against both sets of objectives should be measured on a relatively frequent basis. Within the relationship it is important for both parties to provide open feedback to each other about how they feel the relationship is going. Any such review needs to cover both process issues and outcomes.

The outcomes review at relationship level focuses on the question 'Have we achieved what we should have by this stage of the relationship?' This presupposes, of course, that the pair have openly discussed their expectations at the beginning of the relationship and set some time-lines around objectives – and this is far from always being the case. So an early outcomes review may often consist of no more than asking:

☐ Do we now have clear goals?
☐ Have you already gained some useful learning?

The emphasis lies very heavily on what has happened for the learner rather than for the helper. Later reviews should be able to focus on specific targets – gaining greater confidence, being given more responsibility, a change of job, and so on.

The process review at relationship level measures what behaviours helper and learner exhibit towards each other, and how appropriate these are for the learner's needs. At the earliest stages this might simply be an assessment of the chemistry between the two people – *Are we going to be able to work together?* Subsequently, the review process might measure:

☐ the maturity of the relationship (eg has it become a two-way learning process?)
☐ the frequency and duration of meetings
☐ the appropriateness of each other's behaviours (eg should the helper be adopting a more challenging style?).

The degree of confidentiality about these discussions will depend on the type of development alliance and the co-ordinator's need for specific information to measure the progress of the scheme as a whole. Most partners in development alliances seem ready and willing to provide basic information if they perceive it will be used sensitively and to their ultimate benefit.

At the scheme or organisation level, outcomes measurement must be tied closely to the initial scheme purpose. Typical measurable purposes include:

☐ retention of key employees
☐ improved succession-planning
☐ more people having and using PDPs
☐ improved scores on key competencies within the formal performance appraisal system

❑ (even) changes in employee attitude.

Slightly woollier, but still measurable, are such objectives as people's taking greater responsibility for their own development, or reduced resistance to change.

Process measurement at the organisation or scheme level is largely an amalgam of the relevant relationship measures: frequency of meetings, behaviours, and so on.

Balancing the need to measure (to sustain top-management commitment, protect budgets and maintain continuous improvement) against the need not to interfere more than absolutely necessary is a judgement call. The golden rule is never to measure anything unless you and the participants are all clear about what the information is to be used for and how it will make a difference. Handled right, however, data-gathering can be welcomed by the participants, because it provides an opportunity to put their own development needs (both helper and learner) in a wider context.

The impact on human resources

Very recently, the central HR function of a major UK multi-national canned a software project that would have given all their employees a much greater opportunity to manage their own development. The reason for doing so? The company realised, after some quite substantial expenditure on system design, that employees who were empowered in this way might place significantly more demands on the learning resources available. The department had managed to contain demand up till then by making it difficult for people to match their personal development requirements with those of the organisation. It opted to stick with the current system rather than open Pandora's box, even though it had already raised employees' expectations.

In part, this organisation's panic response was shaped by the fact that it still saw development primarily as the provision of courses. Had it had a more varied portfolio of learning opportunities, with a greater emphasis on development alliances, then perhaps it would have reacted differently. But to have got to that point would have required very different thinking patterns – patterns that would allow them to release much of their control over how development happens. In this case, in spite of a name-change to HR, the function had never really advanced much beyond thinking of itself as personnel.

The more adventurous, strategic-thinking and aligned with business goals an HR department is, the more benefit the organisation is likely to derive from an increasing emphasis on development alliances.

It is not just a matter of being better able to achieve the list of benefits outlined in Chapter 1. The switched-on HR function has the confidence and maturity *to encourage and allow learning to happen*, rather than insist that it should; to stimulate a climate where people recognise, accept and welcome the opportunity to help others learn; and genuinely to embrace its role as the educator of the line rather than its controller. Where such a mind-set predominates, the learning alliance has a major role to play in supporting HR objectives.

An issue here, of course, is to what extent development alliances should be 'managed' centrally by HR. Practical experience suggests that some central support is essential to raise awareness, help people acquire the skills (as both helper and learner), prevent abuses, put people in touch with appropriate alliance partners and generally maintain scheme momentum. But there has at the same time to be minimum bureaucracy. The golden rule seems to be *an informal relationship within a formal scheme*.

Conclusion

The organisation that has an integrated framework of development alliances within a broader approach to development as a whole is tapping a vast reservoir of change potential – the natural, instinctive power of people's willingness to help others learn. Properly managed, development alliances lead to practical, pragmatic, timely and relevant help for people at all levels.

Of course, learning alliances will happen naturally, just as babies learn to talk naturally. Any parent with a child who has reached the constant chatter stage or the 'Why?' stage is aware that knowing how to talk is only half the battle.

Equally important is developing the skills and sensitivity to manage that innate capability. So it is with development alliances. Very often, people lose the opportunity to forge an alliance because they do not know how to approach the other person. Or they lack the sensitivity to be aware that they are doing most of the talking when they should be listening, or to get beneath the presented issue, or to suppress their own impatience as the learner takes time to get his or her thoughts together.

To harness the power of development alliances effectively, the organisation must both equip people to manage the relationship and equip itself with the resources to manage and support a wide range of diverse and constantly evolving relationships. The greater the commitment and resources allocated to doing so, the more rapid the payback will be, as those who are helped begin to adopt the developmental behaviours of those who do the helping. It is significant that people who have been effective mentees almost always make effective mentors. Similarly, in professional counselling it is generally a requirement that those who wish to practise must first have experienced in considerable depth what it is like to receive counselling.

One of the aims for the organisation of the early twenty-first century must be to create a climate of development where helping others to learn is natural, expected and – hopefully – quite unremarkable. That will not happen with piecemeal approaches. It is time that the learning alliance took its place alongside more formal approaches to learning, as a fundamental driver of business and personal change.

End-note

1 *Making the Match: Software for managing selection of mentors and mentees.* St Albans, Herts TEC, 1998.

APPENDIX 1: POWER IN THE MENTORING RELATIONSHIP

A succinct summary of the types of power within business relationships is provided by Stewart,[1] who describes them as follows:

> The first is the power to reward: to give someone a pay rise or a pat on the back. Its twin is the power to punish: to fire someone, to send him to Fargo, North Dakota, or to put her in charge of 'special projects'. The third is the power that experts call authority. Authority can be specific and specifically granted: the right to sign $100,000 contracts or to approve a package design. Or it can be the equivalent of because-I'm-your-mother power: 'Package colour may be my job, but the boss wants it blue.' The fourth kind of power comes from expertise: 'I know the market research better than anyone – and the research says that red will sell better than blue.' Finally, psychologists speak of referent power, which attaches to a leader because people admire him, want to be like him, or are wowed by his integrity, charisma or charm.

How can mentors exert these various types of power? Clearly, the mentor will not normally have influence over the mentee's pay and compensation, except where he or she is also line manager (in which case, he or she will be acting in line manager, not mentor, role). In a mentoring relationship where sponsoring is an accepted behaviour or goal, there may however be considerable scope for the mentor to provide rewards in terms of putting the mentee forward for assignments that will be career-enhancing. A number of US sources make reference to this as a legitimate mentor role.

In a relationship where sponsoring is not expected or not acceptable, the mentor can still reward by giving praise. Whether he or she may also punish by withholding praise or expressing disapproval is more debatable. This is an aspect of behaviour that does not seem to be covered in the literature.

Authority power may have a number of effects on the relationship. Among those I have observed are:

☐ *an effect on the ability to establish genuine rapport* – A high power-distance as perceived by the mentee (or in theory by the mentor) will tend to make the mentee less willing to challenge what the mentor says, to take the mentor's time and/or to 'speak truth to power'. High power-distance cultures, such as those in Malaysia and Indonesia, have particular difficulty in overcoming the natural deference of the hierarchically inferior partner; mutual learning is therefore less likely to take place.[2]

☐ *selection of mentors by mentees* – Mentees may choose a mentor for his or her perceived power-base rather than for potential help with the mentee's development. Fast-track powerful figures do not necessarily make the best mentors.[3]

☐ *management of the relationship* – Who sets the agenda, decides the frequency of meetings, or decides when a topic has been sufficiently explored for now? The more confident the mentee is within the relationship (ie the more equal the perceived power), the more likely it is to be mentee-driven.

☐ *authority by association* – The mentor's networks may be a significant attraction and potential source of benefit for the mentee.

The power of expertise will depend largely on the goals of the relationship. Within the hierarchy of 'helping to learn', teaching (instructing) and tutoring assume a greater expertise in the area of learning by the mentor. However, a coach, may not be as able as the person whom he or she coaches. The critical skill lies in being able to give informed feedback in an acceptable manner. The mentor, it can be argued, draws upon experience rather than expertise; if he or she has specific and relevant task expertise, that can be regarded almost as a bonus. Even if the mentor has at some time done the same job as the mentee, he or she may well have grown so far beyond it that the details are very rusty. Formal mentoring schemes may place some mentees with mentors who share the same basic discipline, while others have mentors from a completely different discipline, because their learning needs are different.

Referent power appears to be a less contentious issue. Darling[4] describes a number of relevant mentor roles through the words that mentees she interviewed used to describe them:

- *model* – 'I'm impressed with her ability to …'; 'really respected her'; 'admired her'
- *envisioner* – 'gave me a picture of what nursing can be'; 'enthusiastic about opportunities in …'; 'sparked my interest in …'; 'showed you possibilities'
- *energiser* – 'enthusiastic and exciting'; 'very dynamic'; 'made it fascinating'.

Another way of looking at power is by source. Hellriegel *et al*[5] define three of the most common resources as:

- *knowledge* – 'individuals … that possess knowledge crucial to attaining the organisation's goals have power.'
- *resources* – 'Individuals who can provide essential or difficult-to-obtain resources have power.'
- *decision-making* – 'Individuals or groups acquire power to the extent that they can affect some part of the decision-making process.'

Within the mentoring relationship, the mentor may have the *power of knowledge* by virtue of all, or a combination, of:

- *greater experience of the functional area, ie depth of experience* – This would be especially relevant in schemes, such as that operated by the Institute of Mechanical Engineering, where the relationship goal is achievement of certification or chartered status. Within the typology of 'helping to learn styles' the power of knowledge would normally be greatest in the roles of teacher and tutor.
- *width of experience: of business, life, academia* – Implicit here is an expectation by the mentee that the mentor has the capability to understand the broader picture and to extract wisdom from this experience.

□ *width of perspective* – Often called the helicopter view, in organisations it is the ability of the hierarchically powerful to see more clearly the career options within the company, and the manner in which the informal networks and political machinery work.

□ *access to more extensive, more influential information networks* – There is, however, a contra-argument here. The junior peer groups in organisations often create their own networks which are largely closed to senior managers but which are vital in terms of getting basic activities done or planting ideas that can percolate up the hierarchy. The influence of network power on the relationship will vary according to the need or desire on the part of mentor and mentee to gain access to each other's networks.

Logically, knowledge power would tend to be of greatest influence in the relationships where:

□ there is a significant gap in knowledge between mentor and mentee

□ the acquisition of knowledge is a significant goal of the relationship (for the mentee, or for both parties).

Resource power appears to have little influence in the mentoring relationship, except through the mentor's influence networks. The mentor holds the power of introduction, recommendation and referral. The balance of power in the relationship may be influenced by:

□ the manner in which the mentor permits access to his or her networks (ie open and freely given or parcelled out carefully); if the mentor is parsimonious with network access, what does the mentee have to offer to the mentor (eg allegiance, loyalty, deference, humility, respect, etc) to gain access?

□ the power of the network itself (ie its cohesiveness and the individual power of its members)

□ the mentor's standing within the network

□ the mentor's skill in understanding and using the network.

Decision-making power is important in the mentoring

relationship mainly when the mentor adopts a sponsoring (godfather) role, using influence to secure preference for the mentee. This can be considered an extrinsic use of decision-making power.

However, there is also potential for an intrinsic use of decision-making power in the management of the relationship itself. Who, for example, decides:

□ when and where to meet?

□ what the agenda will be?

□ when a topic has been sufficiently explored?

□ on actions to be taken as a result of mentoring discussions?

□ the extent to which the mentee has progressed in achieving developmental goals?

End-notes

1 STEWART T. A. 'A user's guide to power', *Fortune*, 6 November 1989.
2 CLUTTERBUCK D. European Mentoring Centre Conference paper.
3 CLUTTERBUCK D. *Everyone Needs a Mentor*, 1st edn. London, Institute of Personnel Management, 1985.
4 DARLING L. A. 'What do nurses want in a mentor?' *Journal of Nursing Administration*, October 1984.
5 HELLRIEGEL D., SLOCUM J. W. *and* WOODMAN R. W. *Organizational Behaviour*, 7th edn. Minneapolis/St Paul, West, 1995.

APPENDIX 2: SOURCES OF
FURTHER INFORMATION

1   A useful book-list

Mentoring

CLUTTERBUCK D. *Everyone Needs a Mentor*. London, Institute of Personnel Management, 1985 (2nd edn, Institute of Personnel and Development, 1991).

HAY J. *Transformational Mentoring*. Maidenhead, McGraw-Hill, 1995.

MEGGINSON D. *and* CLUTTERBUCK D. *Mentoring in Action*. London, Kogan Page, 1995.

Coaching

CUNNINGHAM I. *and* DAWES G. *Exercises for Developing Coaching Capability*. London, Institute of Personnel and Development, 1998.

LANDSBERG M. *The Tao of Coaching*. London, HarperCollins Business, 1996.

PARSLOE E. *The Manager as Coach and Mentor*. London, Institute of Personnel and Development, 1998.

WHITMORE J. *Coaching for Performance*. London, Nicholas Brealey, 1996.

Guardianship

Regrettably, there is not much specifically on this topic at all. However, on US-style sponsor-mentoring, see:

ZEY M. G. *The Mentor Connection*. New York, Dow Jones Irwin, 1985.

Networking

HAYES R. *Systematic Networking*. London/New York, Cassell, 1996.

SEGERMAN-PECK L. *Networking and Mentoring: A woman's guide*. London, Piatkus Books, 1991 (useful advice for men, too).

Counselling

CARROLL M. *Workplace Counselling*. Beverly Hills, Calif., Sage, 1996.

KAMP D. *Developing Counselling Skills in the Workplace*. Maidenhead, McGraw-Hill, 1996.

SUMMERFIELD J. *and* VAN OUDTSHOORN L. *Counselling in the Workplace*. London, Institute of Personnel and Development, 1995.

2.   *Useful organisations*

Mentoring

The European Mentoring Centre, c/o Association of Management Education and Development, 14 Belgrave Square, London SW1X 8PS. Tel (44) (0) 171 235 3505.
The main source of reference for information on mentoring in employment. Maintains an extensive library and bibliography on mentoring and related topics. Encourages research in mentoring and holds an international conference every November.

The National Mentoring Consortium, Mentoring Unit, University of East London, Duncan House, High Street, London E15 2JB. Tel (44) (0) 181 590 7722.
Links African, Caribbean and Asian undergraduates with mentors from similar ethnic backgrounds.

The National Mentoring Network, Business and Technology Centre, Green Lane, Patricroft, Eccles, M30 0RJ Tel (44) (0) 161 717 3135.
Resource centre for community mentoring.

Roots and Wings, c/o Business in the Community, 8 Stratton Street, London W1X 5FD. Tel (44) (0) 171 629 1600.
Links business people with schools and colleges as mentors.

The Princes Trust, 18 Park Square East, London NW1 4LH.
Mentoring for a variety of disadvantaged groups, primarily young adults.

CPS Mentoring Schemes, 128 Mount Street, Mayfair, London, W1Y 5HA. Tel (44) (0) 171 355 9895.

Helps organisations design and establish mentoring schemes, train participants and measure results. Also provides a 'healthcheck' against global best practice.

The Mentoring Website, Herts TEC, 45 Grosvenor Road, St Albans, Herts AL1 3AW. An interactive site being installed as we go to press (mid-1998). For details call Kim Langridge on (44) (0) 1727 813502.

Coaching
No institution worth recommending above others.

Counselling

The Tavistock Institute of Human Relations, 30 Tabernacle Street, London EC2A 4DD. Tel. (44) (0) 171 417 0407.

INDEX

ability of learners, and coaching styles 33

acceptance of development need 59–60

acceptive awareness, role model relationships 44–5

adaptation, role model relationships 44, 45

admiration, role model relationships 44, 45

advancement, role model relationships 44, 45

advisors, guardians as 46–8

ambition, and role model relationships 40

appraisals
appraisees' acceptance of negative items 59–60
problems of vocabulary 58

assessors, coaching styles 30–1, 33

astute awareness, role model relationships 44, 45

authority power 135, 136

balances between opposites, organisational ability to handle 5–6

barriers to development 125

benefits
of learning alliances 5
mutuality of 4, 38, 91–2

body language 21

brokers, networker/facilitators as 77–8

'buddies' 125, 126

Butler, Jim 28

career-oriented mentoring 9, 11, 36, 87, 135

career planning, counselling styles 63, 64

catalytic helping styles 55, 56

challenging
coaching skills 28–30
'helping to learn' roles 7–8, 9
mentoring behaviours 94
organisational values 6
questioning skills 27–8

change see personal change coaching 18–35
critical activities 19–21
definition and description of 18–21
and development career paths 125–6
differences from other learning methods 11, 12
dimensions and styles of 30–3
directive/challenging nature of 8
distinguished from mentoring 18
learner-centred model 19
resource implications 124–5
skills 21–30

commitment
of learners 60–1
of managers 14, 126–7

computer software 130

confidentiality
mentoring 115
process reviews 131

confirming questions 28

constructive challenge 28–30

contacts, networker styles 77

contracts, mentoring schemes 105–6

control
guardian relationships 36–8
mentees' locus of 97–8
mentoring relationships 101, 102, 103
see also power

co-ordination of learning
    alliances 129–30
coping, as purpose of counselling
    63.
counselling 53–69
    definition and description of
        53–6
    differences from other
        learning roles 12
    dimensions and styles of 63–4
    fit within the development
        framework 119–20
    issues in workplace
        counselling 56–63
    nurturing/non-directive nature
        of 8–9
    role boundaries 54
    skills 64–8
    to encourage self-managed
        learning 98
    use of psychometrics 68–9
critical friends
    coaches as 29
    mentoring behaviours 94
cultural aspects, mentoring
        relationships 88, 94, 136

Darling, L. A. 137
databases
    co-ordination of learning
        alliances 130
    network contacts 80
de-layered organisations 3, 69
decision-making power 137,
    138–9
demonstrators, coaching styles
    31, 33
dependency, in guardian
    relationships 36–8, 50
detachment, counselling skills
    55, 65
developers
    career development of 125–6
    training of 128–9
    see also individual roles
development
    alliances see learning alliances

climates 125
commitment of top managers
    to 126–8
dimensions of 6–7
organisational barriers to 125
personal development plans
    122–3
responsibilities for 121
see also development
    frameworks; organisational
    development and learning
development career paths
    125–6
development frameworks
    119–34
    link to organisational goals
        121–3
    management of 123–32
    role of mentoring within
        119–20
development needs
    acceptance of 59–60
    identification of 19
    recognition of 56–8
    understanding of 58–9
development planning,
    counselling styles 63, 64
developmental mentoring,
    distinguished from career-
    oriented mentoring 9, 11,
    36, 87–9
directive behaviours 7–8, 9, 120
    advisors 47
    coaching styles 30, 31
    guardian styles 39
    models of mentoring 88, 89
    networker/facilitator styles 76
dissent 3, 11
double-loop learning 13
dyadic reflective space 15, 16

emotion
    and counselling 55–6
    and learning performance 56
emotional dimensions
    individual learning
        relationships 7, 8–9, 120

organisational values 6–7
emotional intelligence, coaching
    skills 21
empathetic challenge 29
empathetic support 29
empathy
    coaching skills 21–2
    counselling skills 65
empowerment and disempower-
    ment, guardian
    relationships 36–8, 50, 51
    see also power
energy curve, associated with
    personal reflective space
    15–16
equal opportunities
    and mentoring 101
    and sponsorship 49
errors see mistakes
ethnic minorities, mentoring
    schemes, 101, 141
European Mentoring Centre 88,
    141
European model of mentoring 9,
    36, 87–8
evaluation of progress 130–2
executives see top managers
expectations and outcomes, in
    mentoring relationships
    93–4, 105
experiential learning 96
expertise, power of 135, 136–7
extrinsic perspectives
    coaching styles 30, 31, 120
    coaching techniques 33–4
    counselling 63, 120
    feedback 20, 21–5

facilitation of learning, role of
    managers 2, 3–4, 13–14
    see also networker/facilitators
failures, maintenance of
    motivation following 62–3
Fair Play for Women 43
feedback
    coaching processes 20
    coaching skills 21–5

managers' lack of skill in
    providing 18–19
    see also appraisals
flat structures see de-layered
    organisations

gateways, networker/facilitators
    as 76
goals and goal-setting 81–2, 94,
    95, 103, 113, 121–2, 124,
    130–2
growing, as purpose of
    counselling 63
guardians 36–51
    control and empowerment
    36–8
    directive/nurturing behaviours
    8
    effective management of role
    50–1
    potential abuse of role 49–50
    rewards 38
    as role models 39–46
    role styles and dimensions
    38–49
guru role 8, 13, 37, 49

'helicopter view' 138
Hellriegel, D. 137
'helping to learn' roles and
    styles, model of 7–9, 120
hostility, of managers to
    facilitating learning 13–14
    see also resentment
human resource function 5, 121,
    125, 129–30, 132–3

influence networks 73
influence of sponsors 49
information networks 72–3
intervention, guardian styles
    39
intrinsic perspectives
    coaching styles 30, 31, 32, 120
    coaching techniques 33–4
    counselling 63, 120
    feedback 20, 22

judgements, counselling
　processes 67

knowledge, power of 137–8

Lane, G. 40, 45
learner-centred model of
　coaching 19, 27, 34
learners 13
　ability of 33
　development career paths
　　125–6
　missed opportunities 14–15
　motivation of 33, 62–3
　needs of *see* development
　　needs
　personal reflective space 15–16
　training of, in development
　　skills 128–9
learning alliances
　benefits of 5
　co-ordination of 129–30
　measurement of progress
　　130–2
　model of 7–9, 120
　mutuality of benefit within 4,
　　91–2
　resource issues 124–5, 129–30
　success rates 128
　training for 128–9
learning from experience 96
learning logs 82
learning methods 10–12
learning needs *see* development
　needs
learning nets 4, 75, 128, 130
learning opportunities
　and coaching 19–20
　missed 14–15
　role of networker/facilitators
　　71–2, 81
　role of sponsors 49
learning resources 124–5, 130,
　132
learning roles 1–17
levels of commitment to change
　61

limitations, counsellors' need to
　recognise 54
line managers *see* managers
listening skills 21, 65–6
locus of control, of mentees
　97–8
looking out/looking in 63

maintenance
　of motivation 62–3
　of networks 80–1
managers
　as counsellors 54, 61–2, 69
　as facilitators 2, 3–4
　reluctance to accept
　　facilitating role 13–14
　resentment towards
　　mentoring schemes 110–11,
　　114
　roles and behaviours 1–12
master coaches 126
master mentors 126
The meaning of 'yes' 61
measurement of progress 130–2
meetings, mentoring
　relationships 108–10
meisters, guardians as 48, 50
mentees
　behaviours 98–100
　locus of control 97–8
　matching with mentors 104–5
mentoring 87–118
　behavioural styles 9–10, 92–6,
　　119–21
　benefits of 91–2
　contracts 105–6
　definitions and models of
　　87–92
　differences from other
　　learning methods 11, 12,
　　18, 89–90, 117
　dimensions of 8, 88, 120
　distinguished from coaching
　　18
　evolution of relationships 95–6
　expectations and outcomes 93,
　　105

failure of relationships 106–7, 112–15
formal and informal schemes 100–1, 102, 103
integrative role of 117
management of programmes 100–3
management of the relationship 103–10
meetings 108–10
organisations 141–2
power in relationships 87, 115, 135–9
problems in schemes, causes of 110–12
resource implications 124–5
role boundaries 9–10, 93, 119–20
success of non-directive behaviours 7
top management schemes 115–17
mentors
career paths for 125–6
learning from mentees 104–5
matching with mentees 104–5
professional mentors 116–17
qualities and skills of 92, 96–7, 118
minorities, mentoring schemes 101, 141
mistakes, prevention of
by guardians 37
by mentors 100
motivation
and coaching styles 33
maintenance of 62–3
mutuality of benefit 4, 38, 91–2

National Mentoring Consortium 141
National Mentoring Network 141
needs see development needs
negative appraisals, appraisees' acceptance of 59
negative feedback 23, 24–5, 59–60

negative role models 42
network-mapping 83–4
networker/facilitators 70–86
challenging/non-directive nature of role 9
definition and description of 70–2
dimensions and styles of role 75–8
skills of 78–85
networks
development by learners 83–5, 95
learning nets 4, 75, 128, 130
management of 79–81
opening to learners 71, 82–3
as sources of power in mentoring relationships 138
types of 72–5
see also networker/facilitators
non-directive behaviours 7, 8–9, 120
advisors 47
coaching styles 30, 31
guardian styles 39
models of mentoring 88, 89
networker/facilitator styles 76
nurturing 6, 7, 8–9

objective challenge 29
objective support 29–30
objectives see goals and goal-setting
observation
coaching skills 20, 21
coaching styles 31, 32
opportunities see learning opportunities
organisational barriers to development 125
organisational development and learning
link with individual development 6–7, 121–3
measurement of 131–2
need for purpose 124

signs of maturity 128
organisational politics, need for
    advice on 46
organisational values 6–7
outcomes
    expectations and, in
        mentoring schemes 93–4,
        105
    measurement of 130–1, 131–2
ownership
    coaching processes 8, 19, 22,
        24, 31, 32
    counselling 65, 67
    guardian roles 46, 51

PDPs *see* personal development
    plans
peer resentment at mentoring
    relationships 114
perception management 59–60
performance appraisals *see*
    appraisals
personal change
    commitment to 60–2
    maintenance of motivation
        62–3
    spectrum of 56
personal development plans
    122–3
personal reflective space 15–16
    coaching processes 18, 20–1
personality profiling 68
power
    distance 12, 136
    in mentoring relationships 87,
        115, 135–9
    of sponsors 49
    see also control;
        empowerment and
        disempowerment
presented issues and real issues
    66–7
Princes Trust 141
probing questions 28
process issues, measurement and
    review of 130, 131, 132
professional mentors 116–17

protégés 87
psychometric tests 68–9

qualifications for developers 125
questioning cycle 27
questioning skills
    coaching 26–8, 34
    counselling 65

rapport, mentoring
    relationships 95, 100, 104,
        112, 136
rational dimensions
    individual learning
        relationships 7, 120
    organisational values 6–7
reactive helping styles 55, 56
records of contacts, networking
    80
referent power 135, 137
reflective space 3, 15–16
    see also personal reflective
        space
resentment, towards mentoring
    schemes 110–11, 114
    see also hostility
resistance to development needs
    59
resource issues 124–5, 129–30,
    132
resource power 137, 138
responsibilities for development
    121
results *see* outcomes
reviews of progress 130–2
reward
    of guardians 38
    mentors' power to 135
role models 39–46
Roots and Wings 141

self-completed questionnaires
    68
self-development plans 62
    see also personal development
        plans
self-managed learning 81–2

self-understanding 54, 55, 64, 68
senior management *see* top
    managers
sensitivity to mentoring style
    92, 120, 121
signposts, networker/facilitators
    as 76–7
'sitting by Nellie' 2–3
skills
    of coaching 21–30
    of mentoring 92, 96–7, 118
    of networker/facilitators 78–85
    of questioning 26–8, 34
    of workplace counselling 64–8
    see also training in
        development skills
social competence, coaching
    skills 21
software 130
speed of progress, counselling
    67–8
sponsors, guardians as 48–9
sports coaching 11, 20, 25
stepping in/stepping out 33–4
Stewart, T. A. 135
stimulators, coaching styles 32,
    33
success
    measurement of 130–2
    rates 128

task activities
    impact on learning activities
        1, 14
    step-by-step learning of 25–6
teaching 10–11, 12

teams, facilitation of learning
    within 3
testing questions 28
top managers
    development alliances for
        115–17
    as development leaders 126–8
training in development skills
    128–9
trust
    mentoring relationships 106,
        112
    and networking 73–4, 82
tutorial relationships 11, 12
    coaching styles 32, 33

understanding
    of development needs 58–9
    interaction with questioning
        27
United States, concepts of
    mentoring 9, 36, 87–9
unsolicited advice 47

video feedback 22
vulnerability, and role model
    relationships 40

wisdom, mentoring as sharing of
    90–1
work pressures, effect on
    developmental activities 1,
    14
workplace counselling *see*
    counselling

NEW ADDITIONS TO THE *DEVELOPING PRACTICE* SERIES

Flexible Working Practices: Techniques and innovations
John Stredwick and Steve Ellis

Flexible working practices can make the difference between survival and success. Introducing flexible working practices can help organisations respond effectively to customer demand, cope with peaks and troughs in activity, recruit and retain the best people, and save significant sums of money. John Stredwick and Steve Ellis build on the experiences of leading-edge companies – from SmithKline Beecham to Siemens GEC, Birds Eye to Xerox, Cable and Wireless to the Co-operative Bank – to help practitioners develop effective policies on:

- □ temporal flexibility: annual hours, job sharing, part-time and portfolio working
- □ predicting the unpredictable: complementary workers, interim managers and new forms of shiftworking
- □ functional flexibility: multiskilling, outsourcing, tele-working and call centres
- □ using individual and team reward – competence-based, performance-based and profit-related pay, and gainsharing and broadbanding – to support flexibility
- □ 'family-friendly' policies: flexitime, career breaks, child-care and eldercare
- □ clarifying the 'psychological contract' with empowered employees.

A closing chapter pulls together the different options and sets out the main techniques for 'selling' flexibility to a sceptical workforce.

First edition
344 pages
Pbk
0 85292 744 4
1998
£18.95

Performance Management: The new realities
Angela Baron and Michael Armstrong

All employers need to find ways to improve the performance of their people. Yet many of today's personnel departments are abolishing rigid systems of performance management in favour of strategic frameworks that empower individual managers to communicate with, motivate and develop their staff. Here, one of Britain's best-known business writers and the IPD's policy adviser for employee resourcing draw on detailed data from over 550 organisations – including the latest innovations adopted by leading-edge companies, ranging from BP Exploration to the Corporation of London, and from AA Insurance to Zeneca – to illuminate how approaches to appraisal have evolved and to identify current best practice in performance management. They explore its history, philosophy and separate elements, the criticisms it has attracted and its impact (if any) on quantifiable business results. They also offer practitioners invaluable guidance on:

- the fundamental processes: from target-setting through measurement to performance and development reviews
- performance management skills: coaching, counselling and problem-solving
- meeting developmental needs and enhancing team performance
- paying for performance and competences
- introducing performance management and evaluating its effectiveness.

Throughout, the authors have tailored their suggestions to the practical problems revealed by their research. There could be no better source of support for organisations facing this most crucial challenge.

First edition
480 pages
Pbk
0 85292 727 4
1998
£18.95